Planet Earth

STORM

This volume is one of a series that examines the workings of the planet earth, from the geological wonders of its continents to the marvels of its atmosphere and ocean depths.

Cover
Descending from dense clouds, the funnel of a tornado explodes into a thundering, ragged column of debris as it touches the plains of western Kansas on August 28, 1979. This remarkable photograph was taken from a distance of three and a half miles by a woman just minutes before she and her family fled their home.

Planet Earth

STORM

By A. B. C. Whipple
and The Editors of Time-Life Books

Time-Life Books, Amsterdam

PLANET EARTH

EDITOR: George Daniels
Senior Editors: Anne Horan, Thomas A. Lewis
Designer: Donald Komai
Chief Researcher: Pat S. Good

Editorial Staff for *Storm*
Picture Editor: John Conrad Weiser
Writers: Lynn Addison, William C. Banks, Adrienne George, Kathy Kiely, John Newton, David Thiemann
Researchers: Barbara Moir and Deborah Rose (principals), Feroline Burrage, Stephanie Lewis, Donna Roginski, Judith W. Shanks
Assistant Designer: Susan K. White
Copy Coordinators: Victoria Lee, Katherine F. Rosen
Picture Coordinators: Renee DeSandies, Donna Quaresima
Editorial Assistant: Annette T. Wilkerson

Special Contributor: Champ Clark (text)

Correspondents: Elisabeth Kraemer (Bonn); Margot Hapgood, Dorothy Bacon (London); Susan Jonas, Lucy T. Voulgaris (New York); Maria Vincenza Aloisi, Josephine du Brusle (Paris); Ann Natanson (Rome). Valuable assistance was also provided by: Helga Kohl, Angelika Lemmer (Bonn); Enid Farmer (Boston); Judy Aspinall, Millicent Trowbridge, John Dunn (Melbourne); Carolyn Chubet, Diane Cook, Miriam Hsia, Christina Lieberman (New York); Dag Christensen (Oslo); M. T. Hirschkoff (Paris); Mimi Murphy, June Taboroff, Ann Wise (Rome); Dick Berry, Nakanori Tashiro, Katsuko Yamazaki (Tokyo).

THE AUTHOR

A. B. C. Whipple is a survivor of the 1938 hurricane and of a dozen more that crossed Long Island Sound and hurled into New England. As an inveterate sailor he maintains a serious interest in the permutations of the weather. He is a former assistant managing editor of Time-Life Books and the author of four books in The Seafarers series.

THE CONSULTANTS

Robert F. Abbey is Director of the Meteorology Research Program of the United States Nuclear Regulatory Commission. He is a member of the National Disaster Survey Task Force and a past chairman of the American Meteorological Society Committee on Severe Local Storms.

T. Theodore Fujita, Professor of Meteorology in the Department of Geophysics at the University of Chicago, has done pioneering research on tornadoes and in satellite meteorology. He devised the Fujita scale to calculate the force of tornadoes by measuring the intensity of the damage they inflict. Dr. Fujita is the recipient of many awards and citations in his field.

Robert J. Simpson is Professor of Environmental Sciences at the University of Virginia. He has worked in the field of hurricane and typhoon research as a forecaster, a research meteorologist and as Director of the National Hurricane Center of the National Oceanic and Atmospheric Administration.

ISBN 0 7054 0743 8

TIME-LIFE is a trademark of Time Incorporated U.S.A.

XXXXXXXXXXXXXX

CONTENTS

THE MENACE AND MARVEL OF STORMS

Man lives at the bottom of a dense and turbulent sea of gases. This mix of nitrogen, oxygen, argon and carbon dioxide collectively known as air is perhaps 10 miles deep and is perpetually in motion, with tremendous eddies and currents swirling and flowing at different speeds, pressures and temperatures. Frequently, when volatile air masses collide or otherwise interact, storms sweep across the earth's surface; each day thousands of tempests of one sort or another vent their fury around the globe.

A single thunderstorm can release 125 million gallons of water and discharge enough heat to supply the entire United States with electrical power for 20 minutes. A full-blown hurricane will multiply these values an astronomical 12,000 times.

In their terrible power, storms have built frightful records of death and destruction. In Bangladesh in 1970, a tropical cyclone with flooding rain and 120-mile-per-hour winds claimed 300,000 lives. Yet storms are vital cogs in the earth's great engine. They are the planet's air conditioners, continually exchanging warm air from the tropics for cool air from polar regions. Storm winds cleanse noxious pollutants from the air, and rain clouds transport life-sustaining water to parched regions.

Though mankind has forever suffered and profited from storms, only recently have scientists begun to understand their workings. The first clues followed the invention of the thermometer and barometer in the 17th Century. Today, aircraft and satellites track storms a-borning in the farthest reaches of the planet, and high-speed computers assemble enormous banks of data to assist in forecasting.

The more meteorologists learn about storms, the more they appreciate their phenomenal complexity. A typhoon sweeping across the Pacific may affect a million cubic miles of atmosphere in so many different ways that even the most sophisticated computer is at a loss to sort everything out.

In describing nature's great flux, the Greek philosopher Heraclitus noted that a man could never step twice into the same river. So it is with storms, forever assuming new identities, forever exciting man's wonder and dread.

In a spectacular accompaniment to a thunderstorm, a long low cloud pregnant with rain rolls across Patrick Air Force Base at Cape Canaveral in Florida. The cloud's gray black hue is the result of strong cold-air undercurrents forcing the rapid condensation of moisture in the warmer air above.

Driven by the winds of Hurricane Betsy in 1965, the Atlantic Ocean surges over Florida's coast at Biscayne Bay. After crossing Florida, Betsy lashed Louisiana with enormous waves and peak winds of 136 mph, causing $1.4 billion in damage.

Gale-force 45-mph winds and 20-foot waves batter
the oil tanker *Chikaskia* as she pounds through
the North Atlantic in April 1968. Such widespread
and long-lasting storms in the higher latitudes
can generate more power than a hurricane.

A PREVIEW OF THE END OF THE WORLD

The first word of the monster storm came from the Brazilian freighter *Alegrete*, pounding through heavy seas 350 miles northeast of Puerto Rico on the evening of September 16, 1938. As the steadily rising winds topped 75 miles per hour and the ship's barometer plunged to a reading of 28.31 inches, the captain of the *Alegrete* ordered a change in course to escape the full fury of the storm. At the same time he flashed a message for relay to the United States Weather Bureau office in Jacksonville, Florida: A hurricane was building up in the Atlantic Ocean.

During the hurricane season—from June to November—the weather bureau maintained a round-the-clock alert for threatening storms, and operated a communications network of teleprinters linking 15 coastal cities along the Gulf of Mexico and the southern Atlantic seaboard states. As soon as reports from the *Alegrete* and other ships began coming in, the Jacksonville forecaster activated the network with a hurricane advisory—notification that a dangerous hurricane was in existence.

The wisdom of issuing the preliminary advisory was confirmed shortly thereafter. As the great storm whirled westward into the coastal sea-lanes, more and more ships began to encounter hurricane-force winds. The forecasters at the Jacksonville weather bureau plotted the times and locations of the mariners' reports; the meteorologists determined that the storm was moving at a speed of 20 miles per hour—much faster than usual—and that it was headed straight for Florida. Continuing on its present course, it would make its landfall in the vicinity of Miami on the evening of September 20. Now the forecasters issued an out-and-out hurricane warning, calling for emergency action in order to prepare for the onslaught.

During the previous decade Florida had been hit by 11 full hurricanes and another 10 storms of near-hurricane strength, and Floridians knew how to respond to a hurricane warning. Throughout Monday, the 19th of September, shopkeepers and homeowners protected their windows with storm shutters or wooden planks, fishermen and pleasure-boat owners put out additional anchors and lashed down their gear, veterans of past hurricanes checked their food supplies and their radio and flashlight batteries and provided reserves of drinking water, the Red Cross organized emergency relief centers and many visitors from the northeastern United States ended their vacations abruptly and headed home.

By Monday night, however, the hurricane had shifted course. It was now traveling almost due north and was brushing past the Bahamas on a course roughly parallel to the U.S. coastline. At the Jacksonville weather bureau, the

Ripped loose by 90-mile-an-hour gusts in the great hurricane of 1938, a 165-foot church steeple topples onto the main street of Danielson, Connecticut, 35 miles inland from the storm's landfall. The wind and torrential rain of this hurricane, the worst to hit New England in more than 100 years, were so vicious that two men had to hold the photographer upright while he snapped this picture.

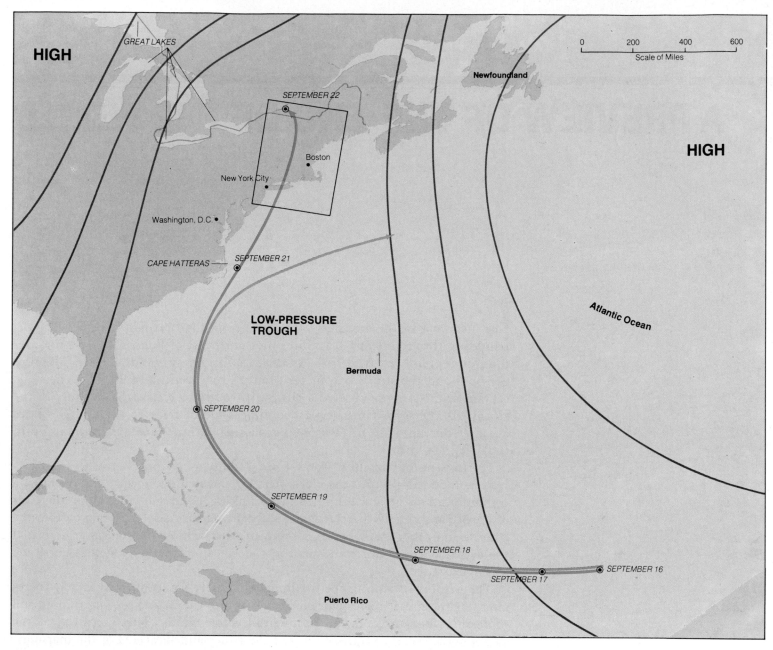

forecasters breathed a sigh of relief. The storm was following a familiar, and relatively harmless, pattern.

The forecasters knew that the great storms had their genesis somewhere in the Atlantic Ocean north of the Equator. From there, the hurricanes responded to prevailing wind patterns, following a westward path toward the United States mainland until the winds steered them north. Sometimes the storms were in the western Caribbean or the Gulf of Mexico before they veered north, in which case they came ashore along the Gulf Coast as far west as Texas. However, when the northward turn occurred while the hurricane was still northeast of the Caribbean islands, the chances were good that the Atlantic coasts of Florida, Georgia and the Carolinas would escape with no more than a glancing blow. And it was a virtual certainty that when the storms reached the vicinity of Cape Hatteras they would move northeastward out into the Atlantic Ocean and gradually dissipate over the chill waters. Thus when it became evident on Tuesday, September 20, that the hurricane had turned north well off the U.S. coast, the inhabitants of Florida relaxed—and so did practically everyone else. There was no reason to suppose that any more would be heard from this ferocious storm.

For a time that was the case. Most shipping had fled the area. The few

According to weather bureau forecasts, the 1938 hurricane should have followed a parabola (*orange line*), sweeping westward toward the Florida coast, then north to Cape Hatteras, where it would finally swing out to sea. But the hurricane's overall steering mechanism, a huge high-pressure center in the mid-Atlantic, had grown extremely strong and had drifted nearly 1,000 miles to the north. As a result, the hurricane shot due north (*green line*) to its Long Island landfall along a low-pressure trough between the Atlantic high-pressure area and a second strong high over the Great Lakes.

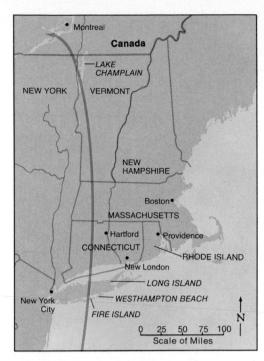

The 1938 hurricane carved a swath of destruction
325 miles long, from the beach resorts of
Long Island through the heart of New England to
Montreal and the hinterlands of Canada. Though
the worst of the storm was confined to a path
100 miles wide, hurricane-force winds of 75 mph
reached all the way from New York to Boston.

reports reaching Jacksonville indicated that the hurricane's forward movement
had slowed to about 15 miles per hour and that it was following the normal
path leading out to sea. By late Tuesday, the hurricane was approaching the
latitude of Cape Hatteras, and Jacksonville would soon hand over tracking and
forecasting to the weather bureau's Washington, D.C., headquarters, which
had responsibility for the central Atlantic and New England states. Jacksonville
advised Washington that the storm still held hurricane-force winds, but posed
no danger to coastal areas.

The weather bureau meteorologists in the Washington office, who prepared
the national weather forecasts for Wednesday, September 21, found nothing
in their data to contradict Jacksonville's assessment of the storm. Most of the
continental United States was basking under the influence of a fair-weather
high-pressure system whose central ridge of dense, dry air stretched from Lake
Superior to southern Missouri. East of the Allegheny Mountains, most of the
Atlantic seaboard states were under the influence of a trough of low pressure,
with warm, muggy weather. It had been raining in New England for four
days, and the forecasters saw more of the same in prospect for Wednesday, the
21st of September.

The weather map that accompanied the national forecast showed no full-blown
hurricane at all. Anticipating the storm's demise, the forecasters had down-
graded it to a mere low-pressure area described as a "tropical disturbance,"
with "winds of hurricane force" near the center. The storm, said the weathermen, "was expected to progress generally northward to northeastward fairly
well off the Atlantic seaboard." After four days of urgent advisories from the
Jacksonville office, the calm tone of dismissal in Wednesday's forecasts was
greatly reassuring.

On Wednesday *The New York Times* published an editorial praising the work
of the weather bureau in tracking "the cyclone that happily spared our southern
coast. If New York and the rest of the world have been so well informed about
the cyclone, it is because of an admirably organized meteorological service.
Hour by hour a cyclone is watched, peril that it is, until at last it whirls out
into the Atlantic."

In actual fact, after early Wednesday morning, no one was watching the peril
that was still roaring along off Cape Hatteras. Not a single ship remained to
report, and the weather bureau was blind to the storm's actions. The forecasters did not know that the hurricane's winds were mounting to a fantastic
120 miles per hour. And they did not dream that the storm, instead of curling
out to sea, was continuing to head straight north. Nor was its forward speed
gradually decreasing as expected. Quite the reverse. The speed was accelerating
until at one point, as later calculated, the hurricane was moving at a phenomenal 70 miles per hour. Hour after hour the maelstrom of churning water
and screaming wind was secretly and relentlessly bearing down on the heart
of New England.

New England, totally unaware of its predicament, had an unprecedented
ordeal in store. This storm would be the first hurricane to strike at the thickly
populated northeastern United States in modern times, and the memory of it
would be seared into the national consciousness for many decades to come.
It would bring some of the highest winds ever recorded on the North American
continent. These awful winds would terrify people and disrupt their lives in a
great seaward swath stretching from New York City to Boston, and from the
Atlantic coast inland as far north as Montreal. Yet, paradoxically, the most
dangerous menace that the hurricane of 1938 bore as it secretly approached the
New England coast was not its roaring winds, but the bulging swell of ocean
it carried at its heart, an upwelling wall of water that the monster storm shoved
along with all its furious energies.

It is the wind that people fear, but with all hurricanes it is the water—the wind-driven storm surge smashing onto and over the besieged coast—that kills most of the people and does most of the damage. So it would be in New England. All told, an area of 39,000 square miles would be savaged by the hurricane. But the residents of coastal Long Island, Connecticut and Rhode Island would bear the brunt of the onslaught and the greatest share of the suffering.

No one had witnessed the birth of this storm, and no one in 1938 understood its nature well enough to forecast its movements except on the basis of past experience. When it was over, the experts would review what they did know, and would add to their understanding the painful lessons of September 21. Then they would set to work to make sure that such a surprise never came their way again.

The experts would explain that, as happened several times a year during the hurricane season, a complicated set of meteorological circumstances had come together near the Cape Verde Islands, in the warm air of the doldrums—the relatively calm reaches of the Atlantic Ocean south of the Tropic of Cancer. They did not know all the circumstances, but they did know the results: In a relatively small area, air made lighter by heat and by an infusion of water vapor, and set in motion by some kind of turbulence, had begun to rise rapidly. The rising air left behind it a low-pressure area that drew more air in along the surface of the ocean, to become further moistened and warmed, and in turn to soar skyward.

The rising air had gradually cooled until, with much of its water vapor condensed into cloud, it had spread outward and sunk toward the sea again. The central column of upwelling air had begun to act something like a chimney, pulling in a draft at the bottom from an ever-widening area and spewing warm air and moisture upward like smoke. So long as there was a source of warmth and moisture at the center of the storm, the process continued and accelerated.

The air being drawn toward the deepening low-pressure area had not traveled in a straight line; forces exerted on it by the spinning of the earth had caused the air to spiral inward, in a counterclockwise direction. When it reached the central area of the storm where the converging winds began their upward journey, the air no longer traveled laterally but spiraled higher and higher around an area of relative calm located in the eye of the vortex. With the inward-wheeling air being transformed into a freshening wind, with whorls of gathering clouds darkening the sky and more clouds towering around the calm eye of the storm, the growing whirlwind had moved ponderously into the path of the easterly trade winds.

These winds were the product of a clockwise circulation around the Bermuda High—a mass of dense, dry air that is always found in the North Atlantic. Just as air in the Northern Hemisphere is drawn inward in a counterclockwise fashion to a low-pressure area, it is pushed outward, clockwise, from a high. The Bermuda High is at full strength during the hurricane season, and the fresh easterlies soon enveloped the intensifying storm of 1938, and nudged it westward toward Florida and its encounter with the *Alegrete*.

Ordinarily at that time of year, the meteorologists later explained, the Bermuda High is centered in the middle of the ocean between Bermuda and the Azores. From that position, the same circulation that aims nascent hurricanes at the United States mainland wheels them to the north as they approach the Caribbean and to the east as they near the latitude of Cape Hatteras. As they leave the Gulf Stream near Cape Hatteras, they are deprived of the warm surface water they need in order to maintain the upwelling of air at their centers, and they die.

However, this time—as the official weather maps for September 21 clearly

On the venerable 18th Century walls of Market House in Providence, Rhode Island, a townsman marks the 1938 high-water line on a temporary cardboard placard, located just two feet above a weathered plaque that commemorates the storm-surge record set on September 23, 1815.

Before the 1938 hurricane New Englanders generally believed that they were immune from tropical cyclones—a conviction reflected in the *Boston Globe,* which reported that "a hurricane of incredible violence swept New England last night for the first time in the history of this area." But this belief was a tribute more to fallible human memory than to historical fact. There had been a number of earlier hurricanes, and one particular storm in 1815 had ravaged the area in almost exactly the same fashion.

The parallels between the storms are uncanny, even to their dates: The 1815 storm, called the Great September Gale, hit on the 23rd of the month, only two days later than its 1938 counterpart. Modern meteorologists, who have reconstructed the 1815 cyclone from mariners' logs and newspaper accounts, say that its speed, track, intensity and landfall were nearly identical to those of the 1938 storm. And the 1815 hurricane reshaped the shoreline in just the same way: "The sea rose so high that it swept down almost every dune the length of Long Island," one diarist reported.

Though the 1815 storm is presumed to have claimed many lives, there were no casualty lists to compare with those of 1938. But fragmentary reports of the day indicated far more severe property losses than in the later storm. In New England's harbors entire rows of wood wharfs were pounded to pieces, and hundreds of ships, relying only on sail, were hurled hard aground. On shore, according to the *Salem Gazette,* "almost nothing withstood the storm. Stores were falling, buildings unroofing, the air filled with flying fragments, and everything levelled with the ground."

One striking contrast between the two hurricanes was in the attitudes of their victims. In 1938, New Englanders angrily blamed the U.S. Weather Bureau for not alerting them to the storm's approach. But in 1815, the storm was stoically viewed as an act of God—or his evil opposite. According to one Long Island tale, a ruined farmer piously declared that "the Lord was in my field of corn last night." "That may be true," his unrepentant neighbor replied, "but the Devil was in mine."

showed but as no one appreciated until too late—the Bermuda High was not where it was supposed to be. Instead, it was centered a few hundred miles off the coast of Newfoundland, far to the north and west. Between the dense Bermuda High and the equally dense high-pressure area that held sway over the interior of North America lay a trough of low pressure—the one that had brought New England four days of rain—running straight north from Hatteras over Long Island and New England. Everything that attracted and nurtured a hurricane—low pressure, plenty of moisture and warmth—stretched in a narrow, inviting path across the heart of New England.

By early afternoon on Wednesday, the 21st of September, the eye of the storm was bearing down on the middle of Long Island at a sustained speed of more than 50 miles per hour, a speed that would later earn the storm the nickname the Long Island Express. Because of the counterclockwise circulation of the winds, which by then were approaching 100 miles per hour, the storm's forward speed was adding to the velocity of the winds east of the eye—boosting them as high as 150 miles an hour—and was lessening the velocity of the winds to the west. It was a tightly packed storm, with its worst winds confined to an area 100 miles wide. Its intensity was indicated by the barometer readings that were recorded in the eye—27.94 inches, an all-time low for the northeastern United States.

Thousands of buildings, ranging from flimsy cottages to substantial man-

Great piles of debris, the remains of beach-front houses carried inland by wind and flooding seas, litter the landscape at Westhampton, a wealthy resort colony on Long Island, New York. Although the mansion at right appears largely intact, the neighboring house at left was wrenched entirely off its foundation by the force of the storm.

sions, were perched on the barrier beaches just off the south shore of Long Island. The narrow bands of beach and sand dunes backed by wide bays stretched eastward for nearly 60 miles, from Fire Island through Moriches and Westhampton Beach to Southampton. Occasionally over the years some of these structures had been slightly damaged by wind and spray. But not for generations had the ocean itself mounted high enough to do much more than pound at the dunes atop which the buildings rested.

By late September most of the families who swelled the population of the beach communities during the summer had returned to their homes inland. Family breadwinners were back in their city offices, and children were in school. Many of those who remained were servants, elderly retired people, mothers with preschool-aged children or solitary wives enjoying the last few days of September sun. When the winds increased on Wednesday morning, some beachside residents telephoned friends on Long Island proper and invited them out to watch the huge breakers that were beginning to roll in from the Atlantic Ocean.

Among the most popular of the dune colonies was Westhampton Beach. A single paved street, Dune Road, ran along this quarter-mile-wide strip of sand, with 179 houses on a 10-mile stretch of beach. As the storm's center approached the midsection of Long Island to the west, Westhampton Beach stood squarely in the path of the most destructive part of the hurricane.

The ordeal began in early afternoon, and it was the wind that struck first. Garden furniture flew through the air, dinghies smashed into docks, roof shingles ruffled like chicken feathers and ripped away. Windows exploded, doors blew open and the wind blasted through the cottages. Heavy black clouds raced overhead, turning daylight to dusk. Utility poles toppled over, darkening the cottages and sending live wires snaking across the ground. Torrents of rain slashed through the broken windows, soaking everything. The tide suddenly rose to the high-water line—although there were three hours to go before high tide. Then came the storm surge.

One man who watched it coming thought at first that it was a "thick and high bank of fog rolling in fast from the ocean." It was 40 feet high, and loomed above the houses. "When it came closer," the man recalled, "we saw that it wasn't fog. It was water."

The storm surge approaching Long Island was the product of several monumental forces. At the center of the hurricane, the water level had actually risen because of the dramatic drop in barometric pressure: The sea's surface was, in effect, being sucked upward. In addition, the autumnal equinox was only two days away, and the combined gravitational forces of the sun and moon were aligned to produce some of the highest tides of the year—two feet above normal on the 21st. The storm's southeast winds were adding to all this by impounding still more sea water against the coast; the result was a massive mound of water, topped by wind-driven waves, that was racing headlong onto the beaches.

Many of the people along the outer beach, terrified by the fierce wind and rain that preceded the surge, had already fled from their homes. Some had made it across the bridge to Long Island proper; many were too late. Those who were caught in the open by the storm surge were swept before it—along with everything else in its path. A woman who swam for her life remembered later: "When I was in the trough of a wave I could look up and see shutters, chairs and pillows getting blown off the wave tops."

Many of those engulfed by the storm surge were beaten to death by wreckage. Hundreds were injured by nails or splinters projecting from floating timbers, or by the jagged glass in broken window frames that washed over them. By now virtually all of the cottages along the waterfront were in the process of breaking up, and some people were able to save themselves by scrambling

aboard floating roofs or parts of houses that drifted near them. One man pulled himself onto such a makeshift raft only to discover that it was crawling with red ants; the fierce horde immediately swarmed all over him, and he frantically dived back into the waves.

At the onset of the storm, a few frightened residents of Westhampton Beach telephoned the police for help. The town's two-man police force, Chief Stanley Teller and Patrolman Timothy Robinson, responded in their cruisers, but they were halted by high water. Leaving their cars, the policemen waded and swam toward the beach-front houses. There they encountered Mrs. Herbert McCooey and her three children, who were fleeing from their flooded and battered home. The officers helped the McCooeys reach the comparative safety of the house next door, which was still standing.

No sooner had they entered the house than a gigantic wave hit the beach and came foaming over the dunes. The building shuddered and the front door crashed open. With the sea rushing through the rooms on the ground floor, Teller and Robinson helped the McCooeys and 13 other people who had gathered in the house struggle up the stairs to the second floor. They had just made it when the next wave hit.

The whole house lifted off its foundation and went swirling across the dunes. As parts of the building began breaking loose, Chief Teller somehow managed to climb out a window and hoist himself onto the roof. He then helped the others climb onto the roof. Succeeding storm waves washed over the strip of land, carrying what remained of the house out into the bay beyond. For five hours the house floated with its passengers across the bay and into the center of the town of Quogue, two miles away. Finally the improbable raft bumped to a halt and everyone climbed down to safety.

Days after the hurricane, the Atlantic Ocean still rolls through freshly scoured inlets on Fire Island, a barrier-beach vacation spot on Long Island. As the storm's 30-foot wall of water washed over the island, sweeping away 200 homes, it stripped the landscape so completely that Red Cross workers searching for the missing had to use telephone company grids to identify the house sites.

The 19 people aboard the floating house were among the lucky survivors of the storm surge on Westhampton Beach. Twenty-nine people died; their bodies were found many miles away. The narrow beach was virtually swept clean—of the 179 houses on the dunes, 153 either washed away or disintegrated; of the 26 that survived, few were worth repairing. Besides nearly denuding the barrier beach, the overpowering waves of the storm surge washed away most of the dunes and in at least seven places opened passages to the bays between the outer beach and Long Island. (All of the cuts were later filled in, except for one several miles east of Westhampton Beach. The residents of Shinnecock Bay had tried unsuccessfully for years to open an inlet through the outer beach; the storm surge obliged them with a deep channel that was 300 feet wide. It came to be known as Shinnecock Inlet.)

The eye of the hurricane came ashore at 3:40 p.m. over Fire Island and Great South Bay, west of Westhampton Beach, and moved rapidly across Long Island. Many people mistook the relative calm for the end of the storm and came out of their homes to survey the damage, or went to the waterfront to check on their boats. Some of them were still in the open when, about 15 minutes later, the eye moved on and the full force of the hurricane winds, now blowing in the opposite direction, roared in again.

Outside the 40-mile-wide area of momentary calm, the great winds continued to lash the island from end to end without letup. In Sag Harbor, the steeple of the Presbyterian church seemed to lift straight up into the air; then it nosed over and slammed to earth. Over the howl of the wind, neighbors could hear the mournful last toll of the steeple's bells. Nearly half of East Hampton's famous elms, planted before the American Revolution, were blown down. Birds flying at full speed were swept backward. People caught in the open were almost blinded by flying dirt and sand. Near Moriches Bay a man was found dead, clad only in shoes and socks; the wind had ripped the rest of the clothes from his body.

In Greenport, the manager of a movie theater decided to stop the show before the electricity failed and herded his 60 customers out of the theater—just before the roof fell in. A woman seeking refuge drove up to a public garage in Bridgehampton and called to the attendants, who opened the garage doors for her car. The wind roared into the garage and blew out the rear wall. The woman shouted, "I guess I've done enough damage!" as she backed away and drove off into the storm.

One survivor graphically described what he called the "voice" of the storm: "The lowest on the scale was the deep bass of the sea; the highest was the shout of the wind through the trees rising at times almost to a scream; but between them in pitch and exceeding both in volume was a steady, almost organ-like note of such intensity that it seemed as if the whole atmosphere were in harmonic vibration. No sound rose above it. It was something one not only heard, but felt to the core of one's being."

By 4 p.m. the hurricane was racing across Long Island Sound toward the New England coast. The ferry *Park City,* making its 12-mile run to Bridgeport, Connecticut, left Port Jefferson, Long Island, at 2 p.m. and was caught out in the sound. It was the following morning before it finally got back to shore, nearly swamped and without power, its 10 crew members and six passengers scared half to death.

Most of Connecticut's shoreline lay within the protective barrier of Long Island and thus was at least spared the ravages of the storm surge. Not so the coast of Rhode Island. The weather bureau had hastily revised its forecast to warn New Englanders of high winds and heavy rain, but it did not mention a storm surge. And the winds had knocked out communications on Long Island so quickly that reports of the terrible damage wrought by the storm surge did not get through.

Once again, the water struck with stupefying suddenness. At Misquamicut, a vacation colony on the Rhode Island-Connecticut border, "people on the beach were laughing and joking, trying to put up shutters and fasten windows to keep curtains from getting wet," recalled E. L. Reynolds. "They thought it was lots of fun. Then suddenly, before anybody knew what happened, their homes were under twenty to thirty feet of water. Some of the houses just blew up. I saw one leap seventy-five feet into the air and collapse before it hit the water."

Forty-one holidaymakers on Misquamicut's beach, including 10 women on a church picnic, died in the thundering surge. Misquamicut was swept so bare that much of the beach looked as pristine as a wilderness.

The same fate befell nearby Napatree Point, a long, sandy strip jutting defenselessly into the Atlantic. Just before the yacht club on the point vanished, the water cascaded into the building and sent a grand piano flying through the roof. One woman who delayed her escape to watch the incredible spectacle suddenly became part of it: A wave washed her onto the crossarms of a telephone pole. She hung on until the pole began to fall, and then was unable to escape because the whipping wires had wrapped her securely to the cross-arms. Thus bound and helpless, she drifted across Little Narragansett Bay all night before being rescued.

Every building on Napatree Point was washed into the bay. There were 42 people in houses on the point; 27 managed to ride the wreckage across the

Derailed Pullman cars of a Boston-bound train teeter over a washed-out embankment near Stonington, Connecticut, after the hurricane has passed. The wind and waves stalled the train on this causeway, and many of the 250 passengers would have perished had it not been for quick-thinking trainmen who herded everyone into the lead car, uncoupled the rest and edged forward to high ground with the last of the engine's steam.

bay to the mainland two miles away, and the other 15 drowned. As the storm surge swept inland, it left people perched on floating houses and on pieces of debris all up and down the coast of Rhode Island. But these were flimsy life rafts, and often carried their hapless passengers to their death. At Sakonnet Point, where a 20-foot-high storm surge demolished 50 of the 75 homes along the beach front, 10 people hoped to find refuge on the roof of a garage. As the roof was driven across the harbor, it bumped into a fishing boat that was still secured to a heavy mooring. Four men jumped aboard the boat, got the engine started and raced for the head of the harbor. They survived; of the others, one was saved when the roof broke up in the waves, four were drowned and one was never accounted for.

Some of the tales were heart-rending beyond belief. On the barrier-beach community of Conanicut Island, off the coast of Jamestown, Norman Caswell was driving eight students home in a school bus. Four of them were the children of Joseph Matoes, who had realized the severity of the storm and had set out in his automobile to collect his youngsters. Matoes had just reached a narrow causeway that crossed a cove when the storm surge came ashore. He watched in horror as the waves devoured the school bus. Driver Caswell was rescued when Matoes spotted his body rolling in the surf and pulled him from the water. "Please let me die," Caswell pleaded. "I just lost a whole bunch of the kids." He had in fact lost all but one; the four Matoes children and three of their schoolmates drowned. A survivor in a nearby town spoke for all the coastal residents of Rhode Island when he said: "I sometimes feel that we have had a preview of the end of the world."

Two heavily populated waterfront cities—New London, Connecticut, and Providence, Rhode Island—stood directly in the path of the storm, and both were battered mercilessly. New London suffered the double agony of hurricane and fire. The conflagration, started somehow in a waterfront building at the height of the storm, was rapidly whipped along the entire waterfront area by the raging winds. With telephone wires struck down, the fire department had to be notified by messengers struggling through the flooded streets. Fire engines were forced to make wide detours around roadblocks of fallen poles, debris and wrecked houses. One fire company, summoned from the nearby town of Waterford, had to cut through 30 fallen trees in order to reach New London. When the fire fighters were finally able to deploy their hoses, the wind blew the water back on them.

The fire raged unchecked for six hours, and it appeared as though the entire city of 30,000, including the U.S. Navy's principal submarine base, would be consumed. Then the hurricane moved north of the city, and the wind changed direction. The fire was thrown back on itself, found nothing but smoldering ruins to feed on and finally died out. Damage from the fire was estimated at one million dollars.

The cost to Providence was far greater. Though the Rhode Island state capital lay at the head of Narragansett Bay, nearly 30 miles from the ocean, it fell victim to the same storm surge that devastated the beach colonies. Unimpeded by the land mass of Long Island, the Atlantic Ocean rose up and came ashore with terrible force. Breakwater boulders weighing 20 tons and more were tossed or rolled as much as 50 feet. The 71-foot, steel-reinforced lighthouse tower on Whale Rock, near the entrance to the bay, was swept away, taking the lighthouse keeper to his death. As the narrowing bay increasingly confined the mass of water, it rose higher and higher. By the time it reached the head of the bay, it was an enormous, rolling engine of destruction 30 feet high. Vessels and splintered cottages were carried up the bay, spinning in the currents and toppling over the crest of the giant wave. The wharves at the head of the bay were overwhelmed by the onrushing water. Hundreds of vessels were plucked from their berths and moorings and battered against one another and nearby piers.

It was 5 p.m. when the seas reached the city's business center. Office workers preparing to go home looked out their windows in astonishment at the suddenly flooded streets. They later reported viewing scenes both terrifying and outlandish: a blond mannequin floating down a street, upright and pirouetting slowly until a log hit and sank it; a large rat riding a gasoline can; a desk floating down the street, the handle of its pencil sharpener turning in the wind; a man swimming down the street with a girl clinging to his back; a woman climbing atop her car and being swept away; refugees shinnying up ropes let down to them from upper windows; a wall crashing onto an automobile, crushing it and the woman at the wheel.

The water in Market Square, the city's center, reached a depth of almost 10 feet. And the autos submerged beneath its surface added their own eerie touch

A tangled pile of sunken ships awaits salvage along the ruined piers of New London, Connecticut, after the hurricane tore the vessels from their moorings and dashed them ashore. The tempest, clocked at 98 miles an hour before the port's anemometer was destroyed, even carried away a permanently anchored 200-ton lightship, which wound up two miles from its station.

to the scene: The salt water shorted their electrical switches, and in the growing darkness hundreds of headlights glowed underwater and the noise from blowing horns could be heard.

Marooned in a third-floor office, writer David Cornel De Jong observed from his window the best and worst of human reactions to the disaster. First he saw people linking arms to help one another reach safety; then he watched the arrival of the looters. "They came, neck deep, or swimming," he wrote, "rising out of the water and disappearing through the demolished store windows. At first there were few, then there were hordes, assisting each other. They seemed organized, almost regimented, as if they'd daily drilled and prepared for this event, the like of which hadn't happened in a hundred and twenty years. They were brazen and insatiable; they swarmed like rats; they took everything. When a few policemen came past in a rowboat, they didn't stop their looting. They knew they outnumbered the police."

The water did not recede until the entire business district had been inundated to ceiling height. By that time the hurricane was speeding northward up the Connecticut River valley, its still-lethal winds ripping off roofs, uprooting trees and devastating crops. The torrential rainfall that accompanied the storm caused hundreds of streams to rush over their banks, and many valley

On Saturday morning, September 8, 1900, early risers in Galveston, Texas, marveled at a magnificent incarnadine dawn over the Gulf of Mexico. Some might have recalled an old mariners' adage: "Red sky in the morning, sailors take warning." The U.S. Weather Bureau had in fact warned that a heavy storm was brewing. But no one did much about it. Galveston was totally unprepared a few hours later when a hurricane swept through, pounding the city to rubble in the worst storm disaster in U.S. history.

Galveston at the turn of the century was a booming port city with a population approaching 40,000. Miles of wharves served more than 1,000 ships each year; the trade included almost 70 per cent of the nation's cotton crop and 25 million tons of grains.

But Galveston lay at the mercy of the elements. The city had been built on a long, narrow barrier island separating Galveston Bay from the Gulf; at its widest the island was only three miles across, with a mean elevation of scarcely 4.5 feet. Occasionally a storm sent water over the beaches to flood a few streets. Yet no major disaster had interrupted the city's steady growth.

It began to rain just after dawn on September 8, and soon a fierce wind was blowing. Alarmed by the falling barometer, the local weather bureau chief, Isaac Cline, drove along the beach front in a horse cart, urging residents to flee. A number of householders sought shelter in the heart of the city; only a few people actually left the island. By noon, it was too late to flee; both bridges to the mainland were under water.

As the afternoon wore on, giant combers washed away beach-front homes. Shortly after 5 p.m., the wind registered 84 miles per hour on the weather bureau's anemometer. Telephone poles toppled, and debris scythed through the air, cutting down people who were trying to wade to safety through chest-deep waters. With darkness came winds of more than 120 miles per hour. Some houses simply disintegrated; others were blown off their foundations.

Not until 10 p.m. did the wind begin to abate. When survivors took stock the next morning, Galveston was in splinters. Half of its buildings had been destroyed. More than 5,000 people had been injured, and another 6,000 had perished in the night.

Surrounded by wreckage, residents of Galveston survey their devastated city a few days after the hurricane of 1900. In this once prosperous city (inset), more than 2,600 houses were destroyed; an estimated 10,000 survivors were left homeless.

A survivor examines the wreckage in Galveston's shattered port area. Although the docks were on the bay, in the lee of the island, the winds and storm-driven waters tore loose five vessels; one 4,000-ton freighter was carried clear across the bay and deposited on a mud flat 22 miles from deep water.

Like discarded dollhouses, half a dozen Galveston homes lie in a heap where the hurricane tide deposited them. A number of homes farther inland survived largely intact because debris from other buildings formed a protective barrier around them.

Despite heavy damage to its roof, the Galveston Orphan's Home with its sturdy brick construction stood fast in the storm. All of the 50 children who had been sheltered there survived, but nearer the beach 90 youngsters perished when the wooden walls of a Catholic orphanage collapsed.

Its roof gone and its 14 imported stained-glass windows blown in, Galveston's Sacred Heart Church is little more than a shell after the passage of the hurricane. Nevertheless, the church was a haven for 400 refugees who survived the night huddled behind its stone and masonry walls.

Boxcars lie askew and canted at crazy angles in the railway yards near the interior port 20 blocks from the Gulf. Hundreds of boxcars filled with cotton, flour and grain were destroyed in a derailment that stretched for two miles.

Grim-faced survivors lift a corpse from the wreckage several days after the hurricane. Many of the men recruited for this gruesome job wore alcohol-soaked bandannas or smoked pungent cigars to overcome the stench; others drank down bourbon, which was supplied by local authorities.

Awaiting identification and burial, the dead lie beneath makeshift shrouds on a warehouse floor the day after the storm. But proper burial soon proved impossible; as the number of dead rose into the thousands, and daytime temperatures soared, mass funeral pyres were built to dispose of the bodies.

Rebuilding a Shattered City

"We are cast down but not destroyed. Galveston must and shall be rebuilt." So wrote a survivor after the 1900 hurricane, and it was with fierce determination that the townspeople resurrected the shattered city.

Within six days a new bridge to the mainland was completed, and badly needed aid was coming in by rail. Many businesses were operating again in some fashion after a week; just six weeks later 39 ships were counted in the harbor, unloading supplies and taking on cotton for export. The city rang to the sound of axes and hammers as millions of board feet of lumber were salvaged and put to use in new construction.

In 1902 work began on a number of measures to shield the city from the Gulf, including a great stone sea wall 3.3 miles long, which was completed in July 1904. Eleven years later, another hurricane roared in. But the wall held and the city stood.

Jacked up and set on pilings, a Galveston mansion awaits the sandfill that will raise it to a safer level, seven feet above the natural elevation. By 1910, a decade after the great storm, more than 2,000 buildings had been raised in this manner.

Passersby watch as sand mixed with water is pumped from the Gulf to build up the island city. In six years some 14 million cubic yards of sand were pumped ashore as a bulwark against storm tides.

Galveston's citizens promenade proudly along the shore and atop their newly completed sea wall in 1905. Constructed of reinforced concrete, the wall stood 17 feet high and was 16 feet wide at its base; the boulders served to dissipate wave action.

Chapter 2

SEEKING THE WHIRLWIND'S SECRETS

Aristotle may have coined the word—"meteorology," which meant "talk about weather." Strolling with his students in the Lyceum gardens in the Fourth Century B.C., the great Athenian philosopher and man of science mused about the causes of thunder and lightning, of wind and storm, and put his conclusions on paper in *Meteorologica,* the first published work on the subject. Although his views may now seem quaint, they were accepted as gospel for about 2,000 years.

Propounding his "rational explanation of things," Aristotle held that the sun draws from the earth and its waters two kinds of "exhalations": One of them—a cool, moist material—was the source of rain water; the other—hot and dry—was "a kind of smoke" that formed "the origin and natural substance of the winds."

Together, the moist and the dry exhalations made air, which gathered in clouds when subjected to temperature changes. During the process of condensation, the exhalations were sometimes forcibly ejected from the clouds in the form of rain. When this happened in large amounts, vast, wind-blown storms swept the earth. Thunder was the sound made by the wind when, having burst out of one cloud, it bumped into surrounding clouds. Moreover, said Aristotle, "as a rule the ejected wind burns with a fine and gentle fire, and it is then what we call lightning."

To the deductive logic of Aristotle, his student Theophrastus added a long list of natural observations by which, he said, the weather could be foretold. Included in his *Book of Signs* were 80 manifestations that he believed to be harbingers of rain, 45 of wind and 50 of storm. Many were fanciful: For example, Theophrastus advised that "the howling of a wolf indicates a storm within three days." In fact, wolves howl pretty much when they feel like it.

But other omens had a basis in nature. "The plainest sign," Theophrastus wrote, "is that which is to be observed in the morning, when, before the sun rises, the sky appears to be reddened over; and it indicates rain." In nature, a lurid dawn is caused by the diffusion of the sun's rays in air heavily laden with water particles—and modern research indicates that rain does indeed result about 70 per cent of the time.

By thus applying their considerable powers of reasoning to the witnessed workings of nature, the ancient Greeks, both in the principles enunciated by Aristotle and in the aphorisms of Theophrastus, gave birth to the science of meteorology. And then, for many centuries, the infant slept.

During that long slumber, great storms ofttimes changed the course of human history. In 1281 A.D., for example, the Mongol Emperor Kublai Khan, already

Among the earliest of meteorological stations, the octagonal Tower of the Winds in First Century B.C. Athens tried to correlate wind and weather. A roof-mounted weather vane modeled after the sea-god Triton pointed simultaneously into the prevailing wind and at one of eight winged demigods depicted on the tower's façade, each personifying a climatic condition expected from that particular wind. Athenians could also read the time from sundials on the walls below the sculptures.

the conqueror of China, launched a huge invasion fleet against Japan. For seven weeks, at frightful cost, samurai warriors contained the attackers within their beachheads. Then, just as a Mongol breakthrough seemed inevitable, the whirling winds of a typhoon roared down without warning from the sea, tearing the Khan's war junks from their moorings and driving them onto the hostile shore. Only a handful of the 1,000 invading ships managed to limp away, while more than 100,000 attackers either drowned or were slaughtered as they crawled exhausted from the raging surf.

In victorious elation, the Japanese thanked their gods for the *Kamikaze*—Divine Wind—which had saved them. For centuries thereafter, they believed that their islands, under the special guardianship of the forces of storm, were inviolate from enemy attack—and during World War II, Japan's suicide pilots invoked the name of *Kamikaze* in the final defense of their homeland.

Similarly, in 1588 the 130 warships of the Spanish Armada deployed in the English Channel in seemingly invincible array. Hectored and harried by courageous British captains, the great fleet sailed northward, along the English coast, increasingly bloody but still dangerous and capable of inflicting mortal wounds. At that point a five-day storm swept suddenly down on the scene, dashing many of the Spaniards against Scotland's rocky coast. When the remnants tried to escape west around Ireland, a new onslaught of storms finished most of them off. Thus Elizabeth's England once more ruled the waves—with the help of gale-force winds.

The knowledge that storms could shape the fate of nations was surely ample incentive for people to fathom the nature of the great meteorological disturbances. Yet throughout the Middle Ages, a dark corridor of time from the scientist's point of view, Aristotelian logic appeared as a steady beam of light —if only because the means were lacking to demonstrate the fallacies of Greek doctrine.

To awaken the science of meteorology and advance it beyond mere speculation, experiments were necessary to test the products of the mind. Beyond all else, meteorology is based on measurements—measurements of temperature, of the direction and speed of wind, of the pressures exerted by air and of the density and moisture content of the atmospheric mantle that envelops the earth.

Such measurements require instruments, and without them meteorology could become little more than a collection of abstract theories, shepherds' tales and sailors' lore. To be sure, as early as the Fourth Century B.C.—even as Aristotle was developing his views of the world and its weather—a crude sort of rain gauge was evidently in use in India; it was a simple bowl to capture rainfall, and when placed at various locations, it enabled farmers and others to make comparative studies of seasonal conditions. By about 100 B.C. the Greeks themselves had installed a wind vane atop a 40-foot-high tower at the Athens Acropolis; when used in conjunction with sundials and a water clock that told the hour at night, the wind vane could fix the changing winds in a more or less accurate time frame.

But beyond these simple devices there was virtually nothing—until the 17th Century, when an incredible burst of inventive energy in a dying Italian duchy bequeathed to meteorological science most of the measuring instruments that even today remain basic to the study of weather, fair or foul.

As the ruler of the small central Italian state of Tuscany from 1620 to 1670, Grand Duke Ferdinand II was a failure of the first order. Ferdinand was a Medici, a scion of one of Italy's richest and most powerful families. But he was vain, politically indecisive and above all profligate with the family fortune that for three centuries had sustained Medici power. In their days of greatness, the Medici had been merchants and bankers; deeming such commercial activities beneath his ducal dignity, Ferdinand closed down the family's financial enterprises, rely-

Aeolus, the barrel-chested Greek god of wind, unleashes a withering blast from the store of tempests hidden in the long, thin sack that swirls about him. In mythology Aeolus gave just such a sack to the adventurer Odysseus, who almost came to grief when the fearsome winds got loose and blew his ship off course.

Of all the planet's natural phenomena, not one has appeared so perverse down through the ages as the weather. Farmers wishing for rain were bedeviled by searing drought; sailors needing swift winds found themselves becalmed; fishermen praying for calm were lashed by savage gales. Small wonder, then, that the gods invented by early peoples to explain their circumstances exhibited all the ferocity and capriciousness of the weather itself.

The storm-gods were an awesomely varied lot, their shapes and characters limited only by the imagination of their creators. When the monsoon rains began to fall, Wala-undayua, the Australian aboriginal Lightning-man, would rise in a rage to ride the clouds, his long lightning-bolt arms and legs savagely striking the earth. With their more sophisticated culture, the Chinese bound their gods into a complex Ministry of Thunder and Storms, including the Mother of Lightning, the Count of Wind and the Master of Rain.

Frequently, obeisance to the gods meant sacrifice. Mongolians poured precious milk on the ground, imploring the elements not to slay their cattle or destroy their dwellings. Any person or animal slain by lightning was always buried on a platform raised aloft—the intention being to return the spent lightning bolt to the gods. The Aztecs, believing that Tlaloc, their rain-god, presided over an army of dwarflike helpers, offered up their children as sacrifices to replenish his supply.

And yet it was not in man's nature to be endlessly cowed and supplicating. Many cultures accorded their gods a refreshingly human and fallible side. In one Norse myth, Thor, the terrible thunder-god, arrives at a banquet decked out as a bride in hopes of duping the pesky giants who have absconded with his mighty hammer. But when he views the festive board he forgets his disguise and plunges in, consuming an ox, eight salmon, three vessels of mead and every other delicacy in sight.

There was yet another side to early man's relationship with his weather-gods. If all else failed, he rose up in wrath. In Japan, after endless unanswered prayers for rain, farmers would seize a representation of their rain-god and hurl it into the fields in order to give the deity a taste of his own bitter medicine.

Besides producing storms and other atmospheric phenomena, Indra, the Indian god "of a hundred powers," supported the earth, propped up the sky and showered wealth on the righteous.

Fujin, the Japanese wind demon *(far left)*, sends down breezes and typhoons alike from the great bag draped over his shoulders, while Raijin, the spirit of thunder *(left)*, beats on his ring of drums.

The vengeful Norse god Thor brandishes his mighty hammer at the giants who constantly plagued him. Thunder and lightning were believed to precede the hammer stroke.

Frozen in midstep in stone and stucco, the Aztec wind-god, Ehecatl, is portrayed as a dancing monkey. Ehecatl's breath was believed to blow the sun across the sky each day.

Flapping his monstrous wings over the treetops of Taiwan, the birdlike god of wind, Hung Kong, was held responsible by the islanders for the terrible typhoons that swept the China Sea.

Under a bust of the venerable Galileo, Ferdinand II, the Grand Duke of Tuscany and a noted 17th Century patron of the sciences, joins members of Florence's Accademia del Cimento in testing the behavior of heat and cold. The experiment, which took place in 1657, employed a thermometer, a mirror and a basket of ice; it attempted to determine if cold, like heat, could be reflected. It could not.

ing instead on exorbitant—and exceedingly unpopular—taxes to provide for his costly needs. Among Ferdinand's several squandering schemes was one to import camels to replace other quadrupeds as Tuscany's primary beasts of burden and transport. The desert creatures did not, alas, prosper in their new surroundings.

Yet for all his fecklessness, Ferdinand had a saving grace: Himself a scientific hobbyist of considerable talent, he sponsored and supported the foremost scientists of his day and place—and in so doing he helped make a shambles of Aristotelian theory. As the youthful organizer of the Conversazioni Filosofeche (Conversations on Philosophy), Ferdinand presided over scientific sessions held in his palace in Florence; later, he founded the Accademia del Cimento (Academy of Experiments), whose specific purpose was to subject theory to laboratory test.

The undoubted luminary of Ferdinand's scientific circle was the renowned Galileo Galilei, who had originally been installed as Tuscany's grand-ducal philosopher and mathematician by Ferdinand's father, Cosimo II. Now, in the middle years of Ferdinand's suzerainty, Galileo was blind and racked with aches and pains from having been interrogated in Inquisition dungeons for his heretical views of the universe. Released, forced to recant and condemned to spend the rest of his days under virtual house arrest near Florence, Galileo nonetheless remained a magnet that could—and did—attract brilliant scientists from throughout Italy. And so, late in 1641, a young mathematician named Evangelista Torricelli enthusiastically accepted Galileo's invitation to join the ducal coterie in Florence.

Orphaned in his boyhood, Torricelli had been raised by an uncle, a scholarly monk who had taken the vocational name of Jacopo. Sponsored by the good Jacopo, Torricelli studied under Jesuits in Faenza and in 1627 moved to Rome, where he soon made a name for himself as an inspired mathematician, thereby capturing Galileo's attention. Only three months after Torricelli arrived in Florence, Galileo died—and the newcomer, then 33, was named to succeed him as the Grand Duke's philosopher and mathematician. Within three years, Torricelli presided over the experiment that was to arouse the science of meteorology from its long repose.

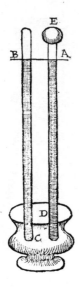

The earliest known barometer, described in 1644 by its inventor, Evangelista Torricelli, consisted of two glass tubes that were filled with mercury and immersed in a basin of mercury. Torricelli wrote that the force supporting the mercury came from "fifty miles of air" pressing down on the surface of the liquid in the basin.

Dedicated as they were to experimental science over metaphysical speculation, Ferdinand's Florentines delighted in nothing more than pricking the bubbles of Aristotelian logic with laboratory tests. During Galileo's lifetime, and presumably at his behest, at least one experiment was devised to disprove Aristotle's axiom that a vacuum cannot exist anywhere in the universe. Around 1640, a student of Galileo's produced a vacuum in a water-filled glass tube, stoppered at the top but open at the bottom, by placing the tube in a cask of water; the water ran out of the tube until it reached equilibrium with the level of the cask, and the space vacated by water was thus a vacuum. In an interesting aside, Aristotle had also postulated that light waves could not travel through a vacuum, but here was a vacuum and it was obviously no impediment to the passage of light.

It was partly in quest of yet another technique for producing a vacuum that Torricelli, sometime in 1644, invented the instrument that even today remains basic to the foretelling of storms. The experiment, as described by Torricelli, consisted of filling a long glass tube, closed at one end and open at the other, with mercury, or quicksilver as it was then called. The open end was stoppered with a finger, the tube was turned upside down and placed in a basin of mercury, and the finger was removed from the tube's open mouth. Because of its weight, the mercury might have been expected to empty completely into the basin. Instead, some of the substance always remained in the tube; moreover, its level fluctuated, now rising, now falling.

"We discussed this force that held up the quicksilver against its natural tendency to fall down," wrote Torricelli. "I assert that it is external, and that the force comes from outside. On the surface of the liquid in the basin presses a height of fifty miles of air; yet what a marvel it is that the quicksilver rises to the point at which it is in balance with the weight of the external air that is pushing it!"

Whence came this force to whose pressure the mercury responded by rising or falling within its glass enclosure? Wrote Torricelli: "We live submerged at the bottom of an ocean of elementary air, which is known by incontestable experiments to have weight." That being the case, Torricelli continued, the behavior of the quicksilver could be explained by the varying degrees of pressure exerted by "changes of the air, now heavier and coarser, now lighter and more subtle."

Obviously, Torricelli's invention could be utilized for measuring those changes—and other scientists soon noted that they were related to turns in the weather, with the mercury dropping dramatically before the arrival of a major storm. Although it would remain for future generations to elaborate on the whys and wherefores, Torricelli's device swiftly took permanent—and invaluable—place in the inventory of meteorological instruments. It became known as the barometer.

As a historic bonus, the invention of the barometer helped turn an earlier laboratory curiosity into another tool that was to prove crucial to meteorology. Almost as if performing a parlor trick, Galileo had demonstrated sometime around 1600 that air expands when heated and contracts when cooled. Nearly 40 years later, a witness still vividly recalled the experiment: "He took a small glass flask, about as large as a small hen's egg, with a neck about as long and fine as a wheat straw, and warmed the flask well in his hands, then turned its mouth upside down into a vessel placed underneath, in which there was a little water." When Galileo removed the heat of his hands from the bulb, which was now at the top of the simple apparatus, it quickly cooled and, as the air contracted, the "water at once began to rise in the neck, and mounted to more than a span above the level of the water in the vessel."

Later, either Galileo or one of his followers affixed a scale to the tube so as to measure the degree of change caused by temperature variations. Unfortunately, this prototype thermometer—for that is what it was—proved to be hopelessly inaccurate. Only after the invention of the barometer did the Florentine scientists realize that the open-ended thermometer was sensitive not merely to temperature but also to changes in air pressure. A solution to the difficulty was provided by none other than Grand Duke Ferdinand himself.

Using spirits of wine instead of water as the reacting agent, Ferdinand filled the thermometer with this liquid and then hermetically sealed the open end. Now, although it still responded to temperature changes, the liquid inside the tube remained unaffected by external air pressures.

Interestingly, Ferdinand and his Florentine colleagues also experimented with mercury in their thermometers but discarded it when they found that it did not rise as high in the glass as spirits of wine when both were subjected to the same amount of heat. Not until the early-18th Century would Danzig-born Gabriel Daniel Fahrenheit realize that mercury's lesser reaction was actually a convenience and calibrate his thermometers to the scale by which, in today's usage, the freezing point is indicated at 32° F. and boiling at 212° F.

In any case, Ferdinand II was delighted with his invention. To ensure its use, as well as that of Torricelli's barometer, he established the world's first meteorological observation network, with stations in Florence, Pisa, Vallombroza, Curtigliano, Bologna, Parma and Milan. At Parma, for example, Ferdinand's agent reported that he had received two thermometers and had "fastened them outside two windows, one facing south, the other north, and I am observing them three times a day." Ferdinand himself was hardly less dutiful. "In the winter," wrote a contemporary historian, "this most Serene Grand Duke looks at the said instrument on rising in the morning, and by the observations that have been made he knows quite well whether the cold is greater or less."

The remarkable Ferdinand was also responsible for an advance in the technique for measuring humidity—the amount of water vapor in the atmosphere. Actually, both the ancient Hebrews and Greeks had had a pretty fair notion of the so-called hydrologic cycle, the constant process by which water rises into the atmosphere through evaporation, then condenses and returns to earth. But the ancients were confounded by the fact that at one point during the cycle the water, as vapor, became invisible.

As early as the 15th Century A.D., observations had pointed to the fact that the molecules of vaporous water, even though unseen, do not change into air but remain separate from the particles of air in the atmosphere. In 1450, for instance, Cardinal Nicholas Cusanus, Bishop of Brixen, Italy, told how a hank of wool would gather moisture, and therefore increase in weight, during humid weather; conversely, the wool would lose weight in a dry spell.

But weighing wool was not a precise method of measurement, and true to style, Ferdinand of Tuscany offered a more utilitarian device. The occasion came when Ferdinand considered the meaning of the beads of condensed moisture that formed on the outside of his drinking glass. This, according to a colleague, led Ferdinand "to make an instrument, which was a hollow glass vase coming to a fine point at one end; it was filled with crushed ice, and held with the pointed end down in a wooden tripod stand, with a beaker below. The air that entirely surrounded it began to change to water, which dropped into the beaker from the pointed part." Though it would be some years before the principle was understood, the ice cooled the surrounding atmosphere, which had the effect of slowing the constant movement of water-vapor molecules within the air; this in turn allowed them to adhere more readily to one another, building up droplets, which then collected on foreign objects, such as the sides of the glass vase.

It was evident to Ferdinand that the amount of water in the air might be calculated from the rate at which the drops of water fell from the pointed container. Thus, from the experiment notes of August 27, 1655: "Two vases filled with ice at the 18th hour. One, put in the cellar below His Serene Highness' apartments made 9 or 10 drops per minute. The other in the great hall, made 11, 12, or 13 drops per minute." Clearly, as indicated by the prototype hygrom-

A rudimentary hygrometer, designed by Ferdinand II in the late 1650s, measured humidity by collecting in a vial drops of water condensed from air circulating around a funnel-shaped container filled with ice. The greater the humidity of the surrounding air, the more moisture condensed on the cold sides of the container.

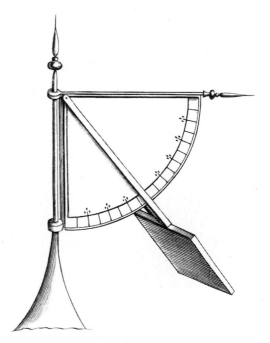

This simple anemometer, introduced by British physicist Robert Hooke in 1667 and used extensively until the early 19th Century, measured wind velocity when the force of the wind elevated a flat pressure plate beneath a calibrated scale. The weather-vane design permitted the instrument to rotate on a central shaft and kept the pressure plate facing windward.

eter, the air in the Grand Duke's hallway contained more water vapor than that in his basement.

In large part because of Ferdinand's many flaws as a ruler, the Medici fortunes fell into such precipitate decline that within two generations of his death in 1670 the family was forever removed from its seat of power. Yet in the barometer, the thermometer and the hygrometer, Ferdinand II, Grand Duke of Tuscany, left to the science of meteorology a legacy of value beyond calculation.

To that legacy was added, in 1667, the anemometer developed by a British physicist named Robert Hooke. Seeking a method for gauging the speed of wind, Hooke came up with a crude but effective instrument: a flat plate, attached to a pivot, swung upward from the vertical when exposed to the force of wind; a scale alongside the plate measured the degree of its swing, and therefore the wind's velocity.

With the subsequent refinement of these 17th Century instruments, meteorologists of the future could at last begin to understand the nature of storms. These would be men with keen powers of observation, with the patience to collect and analyze enormous amounts of data and with the ability to make intuitive leaps of logic.

The voyage of theoretical discovery began within two decades of Ferdinand's death. In 1686 Britain's Astronomer-Royal Edmund Halley, who gave his name to the famed comet he tracked in its course through the cosmos, published a landmark treatise on meteorology after a two-year sojourn on the South Atlantic island of St. Helena. Halley sought to account, as he put it, for the "trade-winds and monsoons observable in the seas between and near the tropics with an attempt to assign the physical cause of the said winds."

Halley's explanation of the origin of the winds began with "the Action of the Sun's Beams upon the Air and Water, as he passes every day over the Oceans." The Equator, nearest part of the earth's surface to the sun, receives the largest portion of the sun's rays; the air over the Equator therefore becomes the hottest belt in the atmosphere that girdles the earth. Warm air, as is apparent to anyone holding his hands over a fire, rises; and cooler air moves in to replace it.

From this phenomenon Halley postulated the vast movements—or winds—of cool air southward and northward toward the Equator from the colder Poles. These migrations of air, he said, accounted for the world's major wind patterns.

But Halley was unable to explain correctly the observable fact that the rivers of relatively cool air flowing toward the Equator progress not directly south or north but instead come from the northeast in the Northern Hemisphere and from the southeast in the Southern Hemisphere. This piece of the puzzle was provided in 1735 by George Hadley, a London lawyer and meteorological enthusiast, whose brother John was the inventor of the sextant. Hadley suggested that the tracks of the winds are influenced by the west-to-east rotation of the earth on its axis. "The air," said Hadley, "as it moves towards the Equator, having a less Velocity than the parts of the earth it arrives at, will have a relative Motion contrary to that of the Motion of the Earth." What Hadley meant was that the earth is greatest in circumference at the Equator and that therefore its surface spins more rapidly at the Equator than it does in the northern or southern latitudes. Because of this speed differential, a current of air moving toward the Equator would always lag behind the spinning earth, and would hit the Equator at a point slightly behind the north-south axis from which it started. With the west-to-east rotation of the earth, the winds would thus be deflected in a westward direction.

Such sweeping ideas as Halley's and Hadley's were directed toward wind patterns on a grand global scale. Nevertheless, it was still generally assumed that storms were basically stationary phenomena, that they began and ended in the same spot and did not travel across vast areas of the earth's surface. It remained for Benjamin Franklin, that shrewd and fascinated observer of nature, to make the connection between wind patterns and storms, and conclude that a storm could travel along a path of countryside or ocean.

At the age of 37, Franklin was well past his days as a printer's devil, or assistant, but it would be a few years yet before he launched his famous kite to test the electricity of a thunderstorm. On October 21, 1743, Franklin was sorely frustrated when a violent storm blotted out the skies over Philadelphia and totally obscured a 9 p.m. eclipse of the moon that he had been anticipating with much relish.

Franklin's disappointment changed to surprise a few days later, when he read in newspapers that the eclipse had in fact been seen in Boston, 260 miles northeast of Philadelphia. On the night of October 21 the sky had been clear over Boston and not until next day did the weather become stormy. Franklin reasoned that the storm had moved from Pennsylvania to Massachusetts, in a northeasterly direction.

His endlessly inquisitive mind aroused, Franklin studied the reports of other storms in various cities' records, and realized that storms did not necessarily travel in the direction of their observed winds. Moreover, he determined that at least in his part of North America these storms moved in a northeasterly direction, while they could exhibit internal winds from a number of directions. Tracking a typical example up the coast from Virginia to Nova Scotia, Franklin wrote: "The air is in violent motion in Virginia before it moves in Connecticut, and in Connecticut before it moves in Cape Sable."

But, Franklin recalled, during the storm on the night of the eclipse the wind had blown *from* the northeast, not *toward* the northeast as it should if the system were sweeping over Philadelphia toward Boston. Franklin puzzled over this anomaly. Several years after the storm that had obscured the lunar eclipse, Franklin was still pondering the problem, writing to a friend that the wind direction must have something to do with a pattern within the storm itself. He was on the verge of discovering the cyclonic form of storms, but he could never quite make the breakthrough. That leap awaited another century—and the work of an extraordinary amateur meteorologist.

This scientist was William Redfield, also an American, and the son of a mariner who had entranced the boy with tales of the sea and its storms. The father had died when William was only 13, and four years later, in 1806, his recently remarried mother moved from Middletown, Connecticut, to Ohio with nine of her new husband's children and five of her own. Only William was left behind; already apprenticed to a saddle and harness maker, he was evidently considered capable of doing for himself.

And so he was. Studying nights by the flickering glow of a wood fire, Redfield educated himself, displaying a precocious capacity for scientific subjects. A Middletown physician, Dr. William Tully, made his well-stocked library available to the youth. On one occasion Redfield borrowed a book in which Sir Humphry Davy expounded a difficult doctrine of chemistry. Redfield returned the volume so quickly that Dr. Tully assumed he had given up after failing to understand the subject; upon being questioned, Redfield demonstrated that he had not only read the book but mastered its complexities.

Redfield was a walker as well as a reader and, as might be expected, put that exercise to excellent use. When he was 21, he hiked to Ohio, where he visited his family, and then back to Connecticut—in all, a distance of more than 1,400 miles. As he walked, he thought about the things he saw, and each evening he made notes on his observations of the towns and countryside he passed through, and on the birds and animals he encountered. Eleven years later, in the autumn of 1821, Redfield set out on another longish trip, this

The Mariner Who Measured the Winds

"Hereafter I shall estimate the force of the wind according to the following scale, as nothing can convey a more uncertain idea of wind and weather than the old expressions of moderate and cloudy, etc. etc."

Thus wrote Royal Navy Commander Francis Beaufort in 1806, as a preface to his revolutionary method of measuring the wind at sea. Like most great ideas, Beaufort's wind scale was simplicity itself. He merely categorized wind velocities by matching them with standard procedures for setting sails on a square-rigged ship.

In Beaufort's scale the lightest breezes, which required all sail just to gain enough headway to steer, were called Force 1. As the wind increased, the ship's speed defined the wind strength until in Force 5 winds maximum hull speed had been reached. Thereafter, the scale followed methods for reducing sail until by Force 11 and Force 12 any sail at all would be carried away.

Beaufort labeled his wind levels with common nautical terms, such as "fresh breeze," "whole gale" and "hurricane." In addition, he used a separate letter code for the notation of other weather conditions.

Though Beaufort's scale had obvious value, more than 30 years passed before it was sanctioned by the hidebound Royal Navy. By then Beaufort had advanced to admiral and chief of the Navy's Hydrographic Office. A superb cartographer, he swiftly transformed this obscure bureau into the world's premier hydrographic institution.

Admiral Sir Francis Beaufort died on December 17, 1857, at the age of 84. But his scale lived on, and in the next decades it was modified again and again to account for advancing technology. When steam began to replace sail in the 1850s, various sea conditions were used to describe the basic wind forces. And with that change from the specifics of a British man-of-war to the general interaction of wind and wave, the Beaufort scale came into universal use among mariners and meteorologists.

Adapted for use both on land and at sea, the Beaufort scale describes the effects of rising winds on the ocean surface and a variety of familiar objects. By matching the descriptions of weather conditions with the wind-speed columns, even untrained observers can estimate the velocity of the wind quickly and with remarkable accuracy.

Cartographer's pen in hand, Admiral Sir Francis Beaufort works at his desk in the British Admiralty in this 1851 portrait. Under his guidance, the Royal Navy's Hydrographic Office won the ultimate accolade from British navigators: "Trust in God and the Admiralty charts."

Set down in a steady hand, Beaufort's wind scale divides all wind conditions into 12 categories. By combining the wind number with the weather code he described beneath his scale, mariners could rapidly log all essential weather data.

Scale of Winds,
Or key to the wind column in this Log.

1 Light air   Or, That which just enables a Ship to steer.
2 Light breeze   Or, That which will impel a Man of War with all sail, by the wind, 3 or 4 knots
3 Gentle breeze   Or, — Do — — — Do — — — 4 or 5 —
4 Moderate breeze Or, — Do — — — Do — — 5 or 6 —
5 Fresh breeze   Or, That which with Royals, &c. may be just carried full & by.
6 Stiff breeze   Or, That with which Single Reefed St. Gt. Courses, jib, & Driver would be just carried by the wind, by a wholesome frigate, then fairly pressed in chase.
7 Moderate Gale   Or, That to which the same vessel would just set 2d reefs St. and jib.
8 Fresh gale   Or, That where the same ship could barely carry 3 reefs St & courses.
9 Strong gale   Or, That when she would break off a lee shore with reefed Courses & close reefed Fore and Main Topsails.
10 A whole gale   Or, That when she could show no other canvas than Storm Stay sails.
11 Storm   Or, That which would blow away any sails made in the usual way.
12 Hurricane   Hurricane!

Key to the abbreviations in the weather column,
in the following log.

b.	Blue sky.	gl.	Gloomy overloaded sky.	p.	Passing Clouds
c.	Clear horizon, distant objects distinct.	gr.	Greasy.	r.	Rain
cl.	Cloudy.	h.	Hazy	sh.	Showery
da.	Damp atmosphere.	hsh.	Hard showers	sq.	Squalls
dk.	Dark heavy weather.	hr.	Heavy rain	sr.	Small rain
dr.	Drizzling	hsq.	Hard squalls	t.	Thunder
f.	Fair	l.	Lightning	thr.	Threatening appearance.
fg	Thick fog	m.	Misty.	w.	Watery Sky.
fog	Foggy.			wh.	White dazzling haze.

BEAUFORT NUMBER	WIND SPEED knots	mph	SEAMAN'S TERM	ESTIMATING WIND SPEED Effects observed at sea	Effects observed on land
0	under 1	under 1	Calm	Sea like mirror.	Calm; smoke rises vertically.
1	1-3	1-3	Light air	Ripples with appearance of scales; no foam crests.	Smoke drift indicates wind direction; vanes do not move.
2	4-6	4-7	Light breeze	Small wavelets; crests of glassy appearance, not breaking.	Wind felt on face; leaves rustle; vanes begin to move.
3	7-10	8-12	Gentle breeze	Large wavelets; crests begin to break; scattered whitecaps.	Leaves, small twigs in constant motion; light flags extended.
4	11-16	13-18	Moderate breeze	Small waves, becoming longer; numerous whitecaps.	Dust, leaves and loose paper raised up; small branches move.
5	17-21	19-24	Fresh breeze	Moderate waves, taking longer form; many whitecaps; some spray.	Small trees in leaf begin to sway.
6	22-27	25-31	Strong breeze	Larger waves forming; whitecaps everywhere; more spray.	Larger branches of trees in motion; whistling heard in wires.
7	28-33	32-38	Moderate gale	Sea heaps up; white foam from breaking waves begins to be blown in streaks.	Whole trees in motion; resistance felt in walking against wind.
8	34-40	39-46	Fresh gale	Moderately high waves of greater length; edges of crests begin to break into spindrift; foam is blown in well-marked streaks.	Twigs and small branches broken off trees; progress generally impeded.
9	41-47	47-54	Strong gale	High waves; sea begins to roll; dense streaks of foam; spray may reduce visibility.	Slight structural damage occurs; slate blown from roofs.
10	48-55	55-63	Whole gale	Very high waves with overhanging crests; sea takes white appearance as foam is blown in very dense streaks; rolling is heavy and visibility reduced.	Seldom experienced on land; trees broken or uprooted; considerable structural damage occurs.
11	56-63	64-72	Storm	Exceptionally high waves; sea covered with white foam patches; visibility still more reduced.	Very rarely experienced on land; usually accompanied by widespread damage.
12	64 or higher	73 or higher	Hurricane	Air filled with foam; sea completely white with driving spray; visibility greatly reduced.	Violence and destruction.

time through his native Connecticut. The trip would earn him a permanent place in the pantheon of meteorology.

Earlier that September, the region had been ravaged by a terrible storm that had swept north from the tropics to slash across Long Island, Connecticut, Rhode Island and Massachusetts. Such storms were frequent in the West Indies, where they were known as "hurricanes," after *urican,* the Carib Indian word for "big wind." New Englanders remembered this visitation with horror, and its effects were everywhere evident. At Middletown, the winds had blown from the southeast, and as he set out on his trek Redfield noticed that the hundreds of felled trees all lay, reasonably enough, with their heads toward the northwest.

Reaching northwestern Connecticut, however, Redfield was astonished to discover that all of the uprooted trees lay with their tops pointed in the opposite direction—toward the southeast. Clearly, the same storm that had brewed southeast winds at Middletown had, only 70 miles away, produced northwest winds. To Redfield, it was only logical to suppose that the hurricane had in fact been a gigantic whirlwind moving slowly from south to north through New England.

But supposition was far from proof. And for the next 10 years—even while becoming the superintendent of a Hudson River barge line—Redfield worked on his idea, analyzing the logs of ships that had been tossed by storms, corresponding with and interviewing shipmasters, tracing wind patterns on huge maps, and trying to make sense of it all. His conclusions, published in 1831 in the *American Journal of Science,* described in compelling detail the very anatomy of storms.

All major storms on the American coast, said Redfield, are in fact enormous whirlwinds, swirling in a counterclockwise direction. The violent winds within a storm move not on a horizontal plane but with a spiral motion, rising from within and descending on the outer peripheries. At the very center of the airborne maelstrom is a calm spot—later described as the eye—that can mislead the unknowing into believing the storm has passed. As the storm's center approaches, barometric readings fall rapidly, reaching their nadir during the calm and then climbing sharply.

The giant whirlwinds, Redfield continued, may have diameters of more than 1,000 miles and their courses across the ocean wastelands can be tracked for as many as 3,000 miles. But the forward movement of the storm as a whole is slow—most commonly around 30 miles per hour—when compared with the velocity of the wild, spinning winds within.

Such revolutionary ideas are often greeted with grave skepticism within the scientific community, and only gain credence after wide and often acrimonious debate. But because Redfield found powerful corroboration from two other scientists working independently, his treatise was recognized almost immediately as a major milestone in meteorological history.

Among those who read and admired Redfield's writings was an Englishman, Colonel William Reid of the Royal Engineers. In 1831—as it happened, the same year that Redfield's first paper was published—a hurricane had laid waste to Barbados, killing 1,477 people, capsizing ships in the harbor and causing enormous property damage. Reid was dispatched to the stricken island to oversee the reconstruction of public buildings and, shocked by what he saw, he decided to turn his life's endeavors to the collection of information about the monstrous phenomena that caused such devastation.

He worked tirelessly, compiling vast amounts of data from historical and contemporary records as well as from sailors who had survived the great storms that boiled up out of the seas of the West Indies. In October 1780, for example, the West Indies had experienced almost a month of fearsome weather that went down in history simply as "the Great Hurricane." So widespread was the destruc-

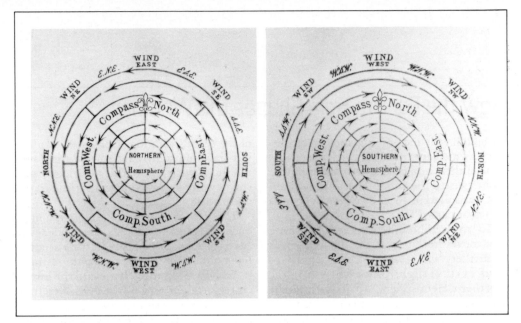

Embodying the principle that tropical storms rotate around a central axis, these 19th Century translucent disks gave seafarers a quick approximation of a storm's vortex relative to their ship's position. All a navigator needed to do was choose the appropriate diagram for the Southern Hemisphere or Northern Hemisphere and align it with his compass heading; the wind direction would then indicate the storm's location. Thus in the Northern Hemisphere, for example, a northerly heading and a west wind would put the storm directly ahead of the vessel.

tion that a British fleet at the island of Barbados was devastated, while a Spanish fleet was cast to the winds in the Gulf of Mexico, more than 1,900 miles distant. But Reid, in a painstaking reconstruction of the events, proved that the great storm was in fact three separate and distinct hurricanes that had followed one upon the other so closely that they appeared to be one mammoth and continuous storm. Thus, though Reid's contributions to theory were meager, his factual findings both confirmed and helped in the further development of Redfield's meteorological explorations.

Similarly and concurrently, Captain Henry Piddington, a veteran of the Indian Ocean merchant trade now on British government duty in Calcutta, avidly gathered information about storms south of the Equator, where, contrary to those of the Northern Hemisphere, tempestuous winds blow clockwise. It was Piddington who pieced together the remarkable—and meteorologically significant—tale of the brig *Charles Heddles*.

The *Charles Heddles*, once a slaver and now shipping cattle between Mauritius and Madagascar, was a fast runner under a hard-driving captain named Finck. On February 22, 1845, only a day after departing from Mauritius, the brig was seized by a great storm, and Finck decided that his only chance lay in running before the furious wind.

Hour by hour and day by day, the storm increased in its violence, its winds veering constantly around the points of the compass. By February 25, her sails ripped away, the *Charles Heddles* wallowed under bare masts and seemed in imminent peril of foundering. Yet somehow the little ship stayed afloat, and on February 27 the sky at last cleared to the point where Captain Finck could take bearings. To his utter astonishment, after nearly a week of being driven by the wind, the *Charles Heddles* lay only a few miles off Mauritius, whence she had begun her wild journey. The rotating winds of the storm had clearly propelled the ship in a circle.

To such storms, Captain Henry Piddington assigned the name of cyclone, meaning the "coil of a snake."

In the meantime, Redfield's widely accepted theory of storm behavior had been called into question by James Pollard Espy, who had at various times taught school in Ohio, Maryland and Pennsylvania before concentrating on meteorology in 1820. During his lengthy career, Espy became known as the Old Storm King as much for his disputatious ways as for his meteorological merits, which were considerable.

How the Earth's Spin Shapes the Weather

Although early meteorologists correctly ascribed wind patterns to the earth's rotation, none of them understood why the spinning globe twisted the wind. That thorny problem was solved in 1835 by a French physics professor named Gustave Coriolis.

To an earthbound observer, anything that moves freely across the globe, such as an artillery shell (*below*) or the wind, appears to curve slightly—to its right in the Northern Hemisphere, to its left in the southern one. Coriolis explained that this apparent curvature is not caused by any mysterious force, but simply reflects the observer's rotating frame of reference—the spinning globe.

The Coriolis effect, as it came to be known, actually combines two factors, one that exerts its strongest force on objects traveling on a north-south axis, another that affects objects moving on the east-west axis. The north-south factor results from the rotational velocity of the earth's surface, which varies with latitude: A point on the Equator speeds along at 1,036 miles per hour, while the Poles spin but do not actually move. Hence an object flying north from the Equator starts with great rotational speed and outruns slower-moving portions of the globe, curving eastward ahead of the earth's rotation. Conversely, an object traveling southward toward the Equator starts with a low initial velocity and curves west, as faster-moving latitudes spin underneath it.

The east-west component is a consequence of centrifugal force, the tendency of any orbiting object to fly off in a straight line unless a force such as gravity restrains it. Gravity pulls directly toward the earth's center, straight down, when observed from the surface; centrifugal force acts at right angles to the axis of rotation—and thus has a sideways component in relation to the earth's curved surface. Since centrifugal force increases with velocity, an object moving due east has more centrifugal force than the earth and curves toward the Equator, while a westward object has less centrifugal force and curves toward the Pole.

Together these two factors profoundly influence the world's weather. The Coriolis effect organizes cyclones and anticyclones (*opposite, top*) and governs the global wind pattern (*opposite, bottom*). Its absence is equally significant: The equatorial doldrums almost never give birth to hurricanes because at the Equator gravity and centrifugal force are perfectly balanced, and there is no Coriolis effect to set storms spinning.

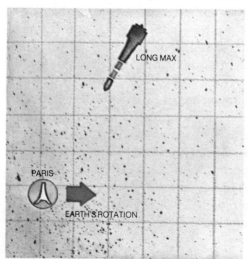

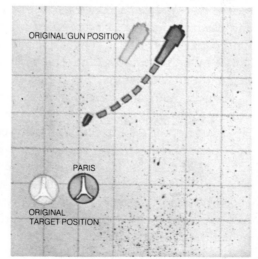

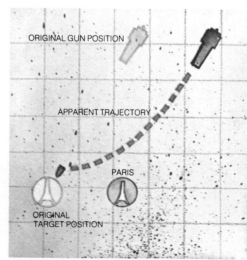

According to a venerable artillery legend, German gunners stumbled on a simple example of the Coriolis effect in March 1918, when they began shelling Paris from 70 miles away with Long Max, a specially built 210-mm. howitzer. The projectiles seemed to curve to the right, just as global winds do in the Northern Hemisphere, and landed .7 mile from the target.

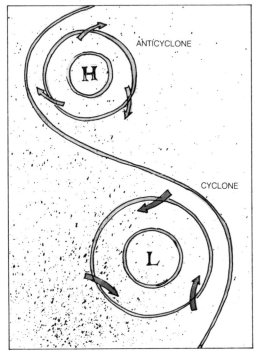

ANTICYCLONE

CYCLONE

Parcels of air rotate around pressure centers because of a perfect balance between the Coriolis effect and the pressure gradient. In a Northern Hemisphere cyclone (*bottom*), a low-pressure center sucks air inward while the Coriolis effect deflects it to the right until the two forces create a counterclockwise circulation. In an anticyclone (*top*), high pressure blows air outward but the Coriolis effect still curves the flow to the right, creating a clockwise circulation.

In principle, single huge convection cells in the Northern and Southern Hemispheres mix cold polar air and warm equatorial air, but the Coriolis effect complicates this mechanism by continually bending the wind in each cell until it blows more or less parallel to the Equator. This divides each large cell into three small ones and accounts for the prevailing global winds. The wind speed is quite variable, however: The easterly trade winds are steady while both midlatitude westerlies and polar easterlies are notoriously capricious.

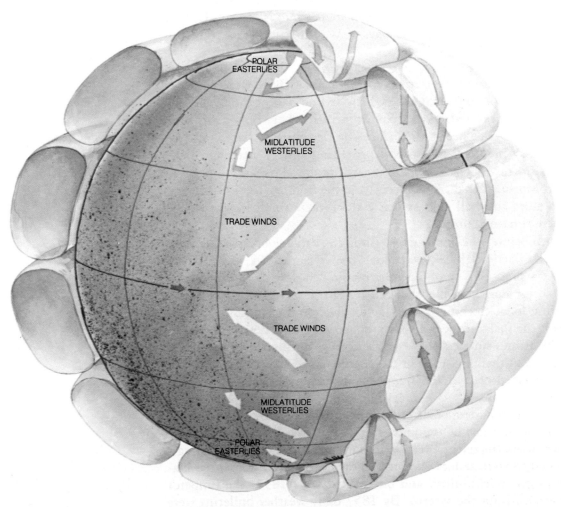

POLAR EASTERLIES

MIDLATITUDE WESTERLIES

TRADE WINDS

TRADE WINDS

MIDLATITUDE WESTERLIES

POLAR EASTERLIES

Where Redfield concentrated on describing the behavior of storms, Espy sought also to explain the causes. In so doing, he developed a theory—admitted by one of its critics to be "beautiful and original"—that held that storms start when moist air, heated by the earth's surface, rises in a column, as if, said Espy, it were "climbing up a chimney." As the rising air cools, clouds are formed and the latent heat within them, when released by condensation, often results in a violent expansion of air—and storms.

So far, so good. Much of what Espy postulated as to the sources of a storm's energy is accepted by modern meteorology. But Espy ran afoul of Redfield by insisting that the gale winds, far from rotating in circular motion, rush headlong and full speed from all sides toward the storm's center. Hailing his own work as "the beginning of our knowledge on the causes of storms," Espy added insult to injury by using Colonel William Reid's carefully assembled data (which had confirmed Redfield's whirlwinds) to refute his rival. Unfortunately, in order to make Reid's facts fit his own theory, Espy was forced to make some glaring omissions and distortions. In his own analysis of the three hurricanes of 1780, Espy picked through the data, accepting some readings and ignoring others, until he could position the first hurricane where the winds seemed to be rushing in toward the center. In actual fact Espy's location of the hurricane was 200 miles to the south of its true position.

Redfield took understandable umbrage, and the two men bickered in print until the end of their days. Both died without realizing that their theories, or at least the best parts of them, were complementary—and that Redfield's whirlwinds and Espy's ideas of vertical convection and condensation as the source of a storm's energy were necessary to a complete theory.

As a footnote to his argumentative life, James Pollard Espy in 1842 was appointed by Congress to become the first official meteorologist to the United States government—and, in the wondrous ways of Washington, was assigned to work under the Surgeon General.

Observation, instrumentation, theoretical formulation—these were the academic ingredients of meteorology as it entered the second half of the 19th Century. But yet another ingredient—swift communication between established meteorological stations—was necessary before the fledgling science could be turned to the critically practical purpose of providing timely warning of the approach of ruinous storms. Already in hand was the tool: the telegraph, perfected by Samuel F. B. Morse in 1844. The incentive came from an 1854 blizzard of wind and ice and sleet and hail that struck Balaklava, a small harbor at the southern tip of the Crimean peninsula.

Less than a month before, the doomed British Light Brigade had charged into history's pages in the Battle of Balaklava. Now, on November 14, as the storm lashed Balaklava, warships of a combined British-French fleet fled for the open sea and escaped, sorely damaged but still afloat. However, 13 transports and supply ships carrying food, clothing and forage for the horses of the allied armies were dashed against the rocks of the cruel Crimean coast. Bereft both of transport and of supplies, the armies suffered unspeakable agonies during the bitter season that followed. Only 500 men had died in the charge of the Light Brigade—but more than 8,000 perished of cold and hunger and disease during the Crimean winter of 1854-1855.

In that tragic occurrence, astronomer Urbain Jean Joseph Leverrier, discoverer of the planet Neptune and newly appointed director of the Paris Observatory, saw an opportunity to use the telegraph as an integral part of "a vast meteorological network designed to warn sailors of approaching storms." He convinced Napoleon III of the project's feasibility, and on February 17, 1855, the Emperor signed the order establishing the system. By 1857 daily weather bulletins were being compiled from the reports of 19 telegraphically linked French and for-

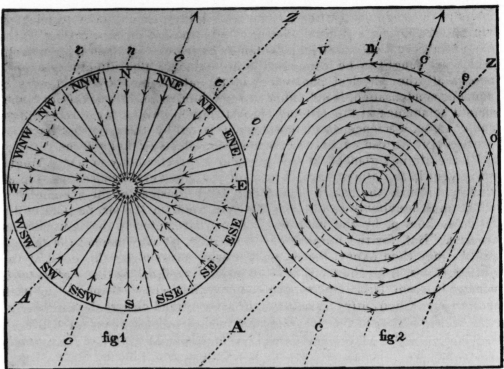

Two early-19th Century American pioneers of meteorology, William Redfield *(top)* and James Espy *(bottom)* waged a heated debate over the behavior of storms. Espy argued that a centripetal acceleration gathers storm winds inward toward a low-pressure center, as illustrated in a scientific journal of the day *(Figure 1)*. The same article pictured Redfield's theory, based on evidence from the West Indies, that storm winds blow in a rotary direction *(Figure 2)*, which proved to be considerably closer to the truth.

eign stations. A similar system was organized in Great Britain in 1860 after a passenger steamer was sunk and 450 people perished in a fierce gale off the coast of Wales.

Meanwhile, in the United States, an infant weather service was already in being, founded not because of any particular calamity but for the general advancement of science and public welfare. In the 1840s, James Espy and another meteorologist, Elias Loomis, had by charting weather data on maps conclusively proved the west-to-east movement of storms across the North American continent. However, this vital information would be utterly useless if it could travel no faster than the pace of a horse or a railroad locomotive.

Samuel Morse's new telegraph was the answer. By 1860, under the auspices of the Smithsonian Institution, no fewer than 500 stations across the United States were telegraphing day-to-day weather reports to the institution's headquarters in Washington, D.C. The Smithsonian did not issue forecasts as such; it merely published daily weather maps. But any astute observer could assume that a storm located over Chicago on one day might hit Boston the following day or the day after that.

The disruptions of the Civil War put an end to the Smithsonian's service—though at least one enterprising individual, a self-styled practical meteorologist named Francis L. Capen, sought in 1863 to convince President Abraham Lincoln that the application of his science to warfare would bring enormous benefits. Alas, Capen suffered misfortune at a critical juncture, and impressed Lincoln only with his ignorance. "It seems to me," complained the President on April 28, "that Mr. Capen knows nothing about the weather in advance. He told me three days ago that it would not rain again till the 30th of April or 1st of May. It is raining now and has been for ten hours. I cannot spare any more time to Mr. Capen."

There the matter rested until war's end and a resurgence of interest among farmers and mariners. This time, a private organization, the Cincinnati Observatory, under Cleveland Abbe, was in the vanguard of the young science. Abbe not only published daily weather maps but for the first time undertook to tell subscribers what all the arcane numbers and squiggles meant—by forecasting what winds were likely to prevail the next day and what conditions might be expected to accompany them. Beginning in 1868, Abbe's "probabilities," as he termed them, dealt with potential storm dangers on the Great Lakes, where winter winds and waves were devastating to commerce. In 1868 terrible storms sweeping in from the west had sunk or damaged no fewer than 1,164 ships killing 321 passengers and crew; the following year, the toll was 1,914 ships with 209 people dead.

So obviously useful were Abbe's maps and forecasts that within two years the United States Congress had authorized the Army Signal Service to build a nationwide storm warning network. Abbe soon joined the new government service and, during 45 years of unstinting and brilliant work, saw it become the largest and most effective weather organization in the world. From 24 reporting stations in 1870, the service grew to 284 stations by 1878. Every station reported by telegraph to the Washington, D.C., headquarters at 8 a.m. and 8 p.m. each day, giving data on barometric pressure, air temperature, relative humidity, wind velocity and direction, cloud cover, and observed conditions of sun, fog, rain or snow.

In the Washington office, a crew of meteorologists swiftly plotted the data on maps and made their prediction for the next 24 hours; if they felt that the information warranted it, they might add an extended forecast reaching out as far as 72 hours. It all happened with great efficiency and speed; the forecast was ready and on the wires to railroad stations and news organizations within an hour; inside of another hour, detailed weather synopses were printed and on their way to 7,000 post offices around the country; and about 500 maps were printed daily for display in public places. Special bulletins were issued for hot and cold waves, for frost, for dangerous wind and for river conditions when rainfall exceeded one inch in 24 hours.

All too often, of course, the predictions proved woefully inaccurate; the state of the art, after all, was still rudimentary, and forecasts were largely based on empirical methods rather than on any true understanding of the atmospheric physics involved. Gibes at the weather service became something of a national pastime. There were further embarrassments when bureaucratic snarls undid the most solid of forecasts. In the early 1880s, a severe frost warning was flashed to Madison, Wisconsin, 36 hours ahead of time in order to save the tobacco crop, which was ready for harvesting. But a telegraph operator failed to relay the message—and the crop was destroyed without warning.

Nevertheless, despite all setbacks, the weather service was gaining credibility year by year, and rapidly becoming an integral part of daily American life. As a noted scientist of the age put it: "While meteorologists cannot tell at what hours to carry an umbrella, they can tell when great storms are coming so as to be of great value to all the industries of the land."

Still, throughout this period of massive government involvement, it is remarkable that the most dramatic early successes in forecasting storms came not from Europe and North America, with their relatively temperate climates, but from the tropical West Indies, cradle and caldron of some of the mightiest atmospheric disturbances known to the planet.

In 1870 Father Benito Viñes, a Spanish Jesuit priest and scientist, immigrated to colonial Cuba, where he was named meteorological director of Havana's Royal College of Belen. And there during the next 23 years, he labored prodigiously to unlock the secrets of storms. His observatory was equipped with virtually every instrument known to meteorology, and Father Viñes invented a couple of his own. Each day the priest took a series of 10 meteorological readings. He would begin at 4 a.m. and end at 10 p.m., and when tropical storms threatened, he would work around the clock. Based on his own findings and on reports received by telegraph from other islands in the Antilles, Father Viñes plotted the patterns of West Indian weather on large charts. He found, although he could not explain why, that the tracks of hurricanes tended to vary with the season; during the summer months, the great storms followed a generally westward

Located in a fashionable town house in Washington, D.C., the first headquarters of the national weather bureau bristles with an assortment of weather gauges in this 1884 engraving. Created in 1870 as a part of the U.S. Army Signal Service, the bureau was officially dubbed the Division of Telegrams and Reports for the Benefit of Commerce, and it attempted to fulfill its franchise by issuing daily weather maps compiled from data telegraphed by observers across the country.

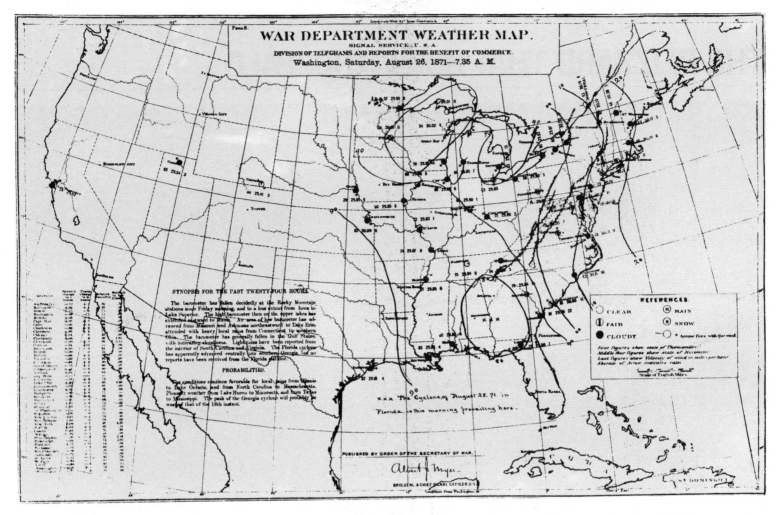

WAR DEPARTMENT WEATHER MAP.
SIGNAL SERVICE, U. S. A.
DIVISION OF TELEGRAMS AND REPORTS FOR THE BENEFIT OF COMMERCE.
Washington, Saturday, August 26, 1871—7.35 A. M.

SYNOPSIS FOR THE PAST TWENTY-FOUR HOURS.

The barometer has fallen decidedly at the Rocky Mountain stations since Friday morning, and to a less extent from Iowa to Lake Superior. The high barometer then on the upper lakes has extended eastward to Maine. An area of low barometer has advanced from Missouri and Arkansas northeastward to Lake Erie attended with heavy local rains from Connecticut to southern Ohio. The barometer has generally fallen in the Gulf States, with increasing cloudiness. Lightnings have been reported from the interior of South Carolina and Virginia. The Florida cyclone has apparently advanced centrally into southern Georgia, but no reports have been received from the Florida stations.

PROBABILITIES.

The conditions continue favorable for local rains from Illinois to Lake Ontario, and from North Carolina to Massachusetts. Pleasant weather from Lake Huron to Minnesota, and from Texas to Mississippi. The path of the Georgia cyclone will probably be worst of that of the 18th instant.

REFERENCES.
○ CLEAR   ℞ RAIN
① FAIR   ⑤ SNOW
● CLOUDY   ○← Arrow flies with the wind

First figures show state of Thermometer:
Middle figures show state of Barometer:
Last figures show Velocity of wind in miles per hour.
Absence of Arrow indicates calm.

Scale of English Miles.

××× The Cyclone of August 25, 71, in Florida, as this morning prevailing here.

PUBLISHED BY ORDER OF THE SECRETARY OF WAR.

Albert J. Myer

BRIG. GEN. & CHIEF SIGNAL OFFICER U. S.

On this early map published by the weather bureau, lines known as isobars connect points of equal barometric pressure in the eastern United States. An isobar of intense low pressure encircles much of Alabama and Georgia, indicating a tropical storm that has crossed Florida from the Atlantic.

WAR DEPARTMENT,
Office of the Chief Signal Officer,
DIVISION OF
Telegrams and Reports for the Benefit of Commerce and Agriculture.

WASHINGTON, March 26, 1873—1 A. M.

SYNOPSIS FOR THE PAST 24 HOURS.

The storm-center, that was, Monday night, over Kentucky, has moved with extreme slowness, and is now apparently over Western Virginia. Northeast winds, with rain or snow, have prevailed over the Middle and Eastern States and westward over the Lower Lakes; brisk northerly winds, with snow, over the Upper Lakes and southward to Tennessee. South and southeast winds, with partially cloudy weather, are now reported from the South Atlantic coast. The northerly winds predicted for the Southwest have extended as brisk or high winds over Texas and Louisiana and northward to Missouri. The highest barometer is central over the Northwest. The barometer has fallen very generally at the Rocky Mountain stations, with cloudy weather, and with rain in Oregon.

PROBABILITIES.

The storm-center move more rapidly northeastward over the Middle Atlantic States on Wednesday. Increasing northeast winds, with rain or snow, continue over the Lower Lakes and Middle and Eastern States. For the Upper Lakes and thence over the Missouri valley, continued cold northerly winds, with clear or clearing weather. For the Ohio valley, northwest winds and cloudy weather, clearing away in the Lower Ohio during the afternoon. Fresh and brisk northwest winds extend from Louisiana eastward to Georgia, with clearing weather. Winds back to westerly by Wednesday night in Virginia. Cautionary signals continue at Mobile, Jacksonville, Savannah, Charleston, Wilmington, Norfolk, Baltimore. Cape May, New York, New Haven, New London, Wood's Hole, Boston, and Portland, Me. They will be displayed at the Lake stations from and after April first.

Published by Co-operation of the WAR and POST-OFFICE Departments.

Albert J. Myer

Brigadier General and Chief Signal Officer, U. S. A.

Daily weather predictions, telegraphed from Washington, D.C., to distant field stations, were summarized in broadsides such as this one for display in rural post offices. By 1876 the weather bulletins were appearing in some 7,000 post offices.

track across the Caribbean to the Greater Antilles and the Gulf of Mexico, but during the autumn, the track quickly turned northward across Cuba to Florida and the Atlantic Coast.

Viñes also possessed rare powers of observation and intuition. He was the first meteorologist to identify a form of high, thin cloud, which he called _cirro-stratus plumiformes,_ as the frequent forerunner of an approaching hurricane.

As the years passed, Father Viñes became famous throughout the Western world for his storm predictions. He made no claim to 100 per cent accuracy, of course, but his predictions, based on past trends and current observations, were close enough to be taken seriously. On September 14, 1876, for example, Viñes forecast a hurricane and described its course; only one ship, named the _Liberty,_ ignored the warning—and came to grief in the storm path that Viñes had charted.

Again, on October 19, 1876, the newspaper _La Voz de Cuba_ announced in an extra: "We have just received from the Reverend Fr. Viñes, the learned director of the Meteorological Observatory of the Royal College of Belen, the following important communication: 'We are very near to the vortex of a hurricane.' " The newspaper quoted Viñes as to the path the storm would take and told how the wind would whip from the northeast, then subside briefly into a calm and finally shift with renewed fury to come from the southwest. It all happened just as Viñes had predicted.

In the spindly person of Father Benito Viñes, no less than in the bustling offices of the great national weather services, meteorological theory and its needful application had at last begun to merge. That symbiotic relationship, in which intellectual pursuit and practical purpose are mutually supportive, each nurtured by the advancement of the other, has been the hallmark of 20th Century meteorology. Ω

Buffalo, New York, holds the dubious distinction of having some of the worst winter weather of any major urban area in the continental United States. The city lies at the head of Lake Erie, on the western edge of the state, and winds blowing along the lake have an unrestricted reach, gathering moisture and strength as they go. Eight feet of snow in a season is not out of the ordinary.

But the winter of 1976-1977 was something to make even the sturdiest Buffalonian shiver. By January 28, snow had fallen daily for 40 days, and a blanket 35 inches thick covered the area. Then a massive low-pressure system sent winds howling down from Canada laden with snow. Though a storm had been forecast, this one struck with a fury never before experienced. Visibility dropped to zero as 70-mile-per-hour winds lashed the city, driving the snowfall in horizontal sheets and sweeping in still more snow from the lake's frozen surface.

So suddenly did the storm hit that 17,000 people were trapped in downtown offices; many more were caught in factories and stores. On the highways, thousands of drivers found themselves plowing into impassable drifts; within four hours, all transportation had come to a halt.

As the storm continued into its second day, volunteers organized to cope with the growing disaster. Snowmobiles were used to rescue people from stranded cars and to carry food, medicine and blankets to refugees huddled wherever they had found shelter. Radio stations stopped commercial programing and broadcast emergency bulletins and messages.

For three more days the winds raged and the snow fell. By the time the great storm finally passed on, Buffalo and the surrounding area lay buried under four feet of snow, with drifts as high as 30 feet in some places.

So severe was the storm that Buffalo and nine nearby counties were declared a disaster area by the federal government, marking the first time in history that blizzard damage had been thus recognized. Despite massive military aid, it took Buffalo two weeks to dig out and total up the cost. The bill for the five-day storm was reckoned at $250 million. The toll in human terms was 29 dead—nine of them people who had frozen to death in their cars.

Wind-blown snowdrifts bury a major highway near Buffalo, New York, as motorists who deserted their vehicles during the great blizzard begin the arduous task of digging out. In all, 5,000 autos and trucks were abandoned during the five-day storm.

After 45 consecutive days of fierce cold, the
famed Niagara Falls straddling the U.S.-Canadian
border show signs of icing over. The American
Falls *(upper left)* are already solidly covered with ice,
while the Horseshoe Falls on the Canadian
side have ice building up in places.

Farm buildings in Erie County, near Buffalo, lie capped in huge snowdrifts piled up by the near hurricane-force winds. Some rural families remained isolated for as long as 10 days.

Buffalo lies still and silent under a mantle of wind-blown snow after the storm. The city government imposed a week-long ban on all but emergency travel to clear the way for snow-removal operators.

An Air Force C-5A transport, then the biggest
aircraft in the world, disgorges a bulldozer at
Buffalo International Airport as part of an airlift of
snow-removal and medical vehicles to the city.
Nearly 1,000 National Guardsmen, Marines
and Army troops were sent in to help clear the snow.

U.S. Army earth-moving equipment works through
the night to remove snow from major streets
in downtown Buffalo. Thousands of truckloads of
snow were dumped onto frozen Lake Erie and
the Niagara River, as well as in parks, where some
of the mounds did not melt away until May.

A U.S. Marine on snowshoes carries supplies
brought in by helicopter to a rural family stranded
in a home near Watertown, New York. The
military services flew scores of rescue missions,
bringing food and fuel to snowbound farms.

A motorist lifts the hood of his car to discover in astonishment that the engine compartment is packed with snow. The raging winds had driven the snow up into the engine area from beneath.

Peering out through a door pane she has cleared, a woman in suburban Williamsville contemplates her snowy prison. A nurse, she was unable for two days to reach her hospital to relieve the overworked staff trapped there by the blizzard.

Grimacing against the blowing snow, a postman wades through hip-high drifts in an effort to complete his appointed rounds. Mail carriers missed delivery Saturday, the second day of the storm, but by Monday they were back on the streets.

Chapter 3

A RUSH OF DISCOVERY IN NORWAY

Vilhelm Bjerknes was 41 years old and a professor of physics at the University of Stockholm in 1903 when he decided to make the study of weather his life's true labor. The Norwegian-born Bjerknes had long been fascinated by the workings of the atmosphere, and now he intended to unlock its innermost secrets. His decision was the cause of some levity and much solemn headshaking at the university. One colleague offered the bleak augury: "He who goes into meteorology is lost."

It was a reasonable assessment, considering the state of the science at the turn of the century. A very few brilliant men such as Father Benito Viñes in Cuba seemed to be making some headway. Yet Viñes' success—in forecasting hurricanes—stemmed more from intuition and empirical knowledge than from any real understanding of the physical processes involved. More important, the lessons of the tropics available in Cuba had no apparent application to the great storms that swept year-round across the temperate latitudes. It was true, of course, that the advent of the telegraph had made possible the establishment of national weather services, with hopes of tracking such storms and predicting their paths. But the forecasts were imprecise at best and more often than not altogether wrong. Indeed, so monumental and baffling were the forces at work in storms that a number of sensible scientists were prepared to surrender to God's will and let it go at that.

But not Vilhelm Bjerknes. He was possessed of an absolute faith in the ability of science to explain all the mysteries of the physical world with mathematical precision. It was merely a question of finding the proper formula.

Bjerknes' scientific creed was inherited from his father, a professor of mathematics at the University of Christiana (later Oslo) and a pioneer in the dynamics of fluids. The youth's love of science had been nurtured by university training in Norway, and later through studies in France and Germany under Jules Henri Poincaré, the brilliant mathematician, and Heinrich Hertz, the wizard of electromagnetism. Having watched these men successfully apply the laws of physics to a wide range of problems, Bjerknes understandably believed that there was nothing in the universe so complex that it could not be similarly explained.

In his investigation of weather, Bjerknes planned a methodical approach. His objective was first to define an existing state of the atmosphere at a particular point in time; he then intended to invoke the laws of thermodynamics and hydrodynamics, and thereby calculate "a future state of the atmosphere." He was not particularly interested in forecasting as such—he knew that by the time the necessary calculations had been completed the weather in question would be long gone—but rather in a total understanding of the physical principles involved.

Vilhelm Bjerknes would never gain his goal; it would still be out of reach for scientists three quarters of a century later. But he would achieve stunning advances in worldwide meteorological practice—advances that rank among the most remarkable in the history of science.

In a sudden creative rush after years of preparation, Bjerknes and a handful of assistants would penetrate as never before into the heart of the blizzards, gales and rainstorms that bedeviled the dense, industrial populations of the temperate latitudes. In a mere five years the Bergen school of meteorological theory, named for the Norwegian city that was its headquarters, would define with unprecedented clarity the structure, formation and behavior of air masses and what Bjerknes and his associates termed "wave cyclones." Their work would have profound consequences for every aspect of life affected by weather. It would be the beginning of modern meteorology.

Bjerknes' project was easily outlined, but not readily achieved. To define a state of the atmosphere at a given time required measurements of temperature, pressure, humidity, density and wind velocity from a broad range of locations. He needed instruments, observers, a central administrative and laboratory staff—all of which meant money. In 1905 Bjerknes visited the United States and persuaded the Carnegie Institution to assist financially with an annual grant that was to continue for almost 40 years. But he did not have the assistants or the facilities he needed at Stockholm, nor did he find them in Norway when he returned home in 1907. In fact, few European nations had the resources to support a research project of the size Bjerknes envisioned, and even fewer had the motivation.

All that changed quite suddenly in 1912, when a country that possessed the resources discovered the motivation. In Germany, the growth of empire and the increasing possibility of war focused intense interest on meteorology as it affected communications and strategy. A specific concern was the new airship line DELAG, whose attempts to inaugurate scheduled flights between German cities were at the mercy of vicious storms. The German government funded an institute of geophysics at the university in Leipzig and Vilhelm Bjerknes was recruited to be its first director.

At last he had all the money, equipment and eager assistants he could wish for. And at first, what Germany was content to accept from Bjerknes—a better theoretical understanding of the atmosphere and a corps of trained meteorologists—coincided with what Bjerknes hoped to accomplish. Results of the partnership were soon apparent. "For the first time," wrote Bjerknes, "we have made headway with meteorological prognosis based on dynamic principles."

Bjerknes was among the first to theorize that the atmosphere behaved like a vast heat engine—converting heat energy provided by the sun into kinetic energy in the form of wind. Thus it acted constantly to move surplus heat from the steamy Equator toward the frigid Poles. By applying the formulas of thermodynamics, Bjerknes was able during his labors at Leipzig to deduce theoretically how certain aspects of the weather would change, and then to confirm the predictions with subsequent measurements. But it took a long time to do the calculations, and that raised questions about their immediate usefulness. "How much practical significance this might have," Bjerknes said, "it is still too soon to say." He was confirming, however, that known dynamic principles were at work.

This exciting progress continued for less than two years, until in 1914 the outbreak of World War I changed the demands on both Bjerknes and meteorology. Instead of allowing Bjerknes to concentrate on broad theoretical principles, the Germans now required precise daily weather forecasts. The pilots of aircraft and airships needed to know what conditions they would encounter on their missions; because long-range artillery barrages could be significantly affected by wind, accurate weather forecasts were also essential in planning ground assaults.

Before long, Bjerknes and his colleagues were totally at the service of the

Vilhelm Bjerknes laid the cornerstone for modern meteorological theory with his discovery in 1918 that weather patterns in the temperate middle latitudes of the world are a result not of changing barometric pressure, but of the interaction between warm and cold air masses.

German military and were chafing under the yoke of wartime exigencies. In these circumstances, the offer Bjerknes received in the spring of 1917 to return to Norway and pursue his original line of research must have seemed a godsend.

The Bergen Museum, located in the principal city of western Norway, was launching an ambitious program to create a faculty of mathematics and natural sciences and a geophysics institute; eventually, the museum hoped to become a university. The organizers wanted Bjerknes to serve as one of the first professors of the Bergen Geophysical Institute and guide it into meteorology.

Bjerknes eagerly accepted, and his 20-year-old son Jacob—who had become deeply involved in his father's work in Leipzig and was eager to continue—soon joined him in Bergen. The city was perched on a high promontory on the western coast of Norway at approximately the same latitude as Anchorage, Alaska, and what is now Leningrad in the Soviet Union. Since the Middle Ages it had been the economic and cultural center of Vestlandet, the part of Norway west of the Long Mountains that formed the backbone of the country. Bergen took its livelihood from the sea, and it was from the sea that its weather—fair or foul—arrived. Bjerknes' goal as he resumed work remained the same that it had been for 14 years—to define and predict theoretically the behavior of the atmosphere. But once again, more urgent needs forced a change in course.

Because of its cold climate and rocky terrain, Norway was compelled to import a significant portion of the cereal grains its people needed for survival. The World War had progressively cut off supplies until, in 1917, the country faced the prospect of famine. So urgent was the need to increase agricultural production that farmers were required to cultivate fallow fields, animals and laborers could be drafted for farm work, and misused land could be appropriated by the state. As the crisis deepened in February of 1918, a newspaper article galvanized Bjerknes into action.

The article described Sweden's plans for a forecasting service to be provided by telephone to its farmers. Observing that prompt and accurate weather forecasts could greatly improve agricultural production, the writer wondered why Norway was not planning a similar service. The writer then went on to quote the director of the Norwegian Meteorological Institute, Theodor Hesselberg, as saying that there were too many difficulties involved for such a project to be practical.

Bjerknes fired off a furious letter of protest to Hesselberg: "I have been disturbed by reading your surrendering remarks," he wrote. "For the sake of the country meteorology is duty-bound to do its utmost. And a situation like the present one for getting meteorology the resources it properly deserves will never arise again."

Bjerknes' challenging letter had a powerful effect. Hesselberg reconsidered, and after discussion with Norway's Prime Minister, Bjerknes was given the job of organizing a national forecast service. "Life is fateful," he wrote a friend. "Now I have suddenly become a 'practical' meteorologist." And with considerable distaste he contemplated immersing himself in a "radically inexact science."

Ever since the invention of the barometer, the onset of storms had been associated with low pressure. The primary concern of the forecaster in the early 1900s was to collect barometric pressure readings from various weather stations and to map the areas of high and low pressure by drawing isobars—lines connecting points of equal pressure. The more or less circular lows outlined by the isobars were known as cyclones—a term that had become generic for virtually all storms. By definition, a cyclone was an area of low pressure surrounded by circulating winds, counterclockwise in the Northern Hemisphere, clockwise in the Southern Hemisphere.

The forecaster assumed that the worst weather conditions coincided with the lowest pressure at the center of the cyclone. His task was to predict the movement of the low-pressure field—and hence, it was believed, the movement of the storm.

Two German soldiers adjust ballast on a hydrogen-filled balloon before launching it from a field weather station along the Western Front during World War I. The path of the balloon's ascent, monitored with a theodolite (left), indicated the speed and the direction of the wind.

Temperate Latitudes, Monster Storms

The great storms that ravage temperate latitudes between the polar regions and the tropics are the largest and most powerful weather systems on earth. Although in many respects they resemble the tropical hurricanes that sometimes invade their domain—both are cyclonic in circulation—there is no comparison when it comes to size; while a hurricane's destructive impact usually measures a few hundred miles across, the diameter of a midlatitude storm can reach 1,000 miles or more.

The range of such a storm can be virtually hemispheric. The same frontal system that in August of 1979 spawned killer tornadoes in America's midwestern and New England states went on to cross the Atlantic and lash the Irish Sea four days later with tragic consequences for yachtsmen participating in the famed Fastnet Race (below).

These tempests of the temperate zone possess impressive arsenals of malevolent manifestations—raging floods, paralyzing blizzards, catastrophic gales, sometimes all three in one storm—and for all their majesty they can work astonishing changes of pace. The Fastnet storm, scrutinized for days, nevertheless intensified without warning. And the blizzard of 1888 (opposite, bottom right) engulfed Washington, D.C., so suddenly that communications were cut off before New York could be warned of the approach of near-zero cold and a 20-inch snowfall.

Despite their capacity for surprise, the very enormity of these monster storms usually precludes the sudden, savage onslaught that typifies their smaller cousins, the hurricanes and tornadoes. Funnel clouds and screaming tropical winds may be the stuff of legend, but the slow darkening of the western sky before the ponderous approach of a frontal storm bespeaks a far grander and more elemental rhythm of the planet.

A huge wave, apparently noticed by only two members of the storm-weary crew, looms behind the 77-foot racing yacht *Kialoa* during the August 1979 Fastnet Race between England and Ireland. Five boats were sunk and 20 more abandoned, with a loss of 15 lives, in the brutal seas and vicious winds of the gale that caught all 302 race entrants at sea. *Kialoa*, which took second place, was one of only 75 vessels to finish the race.

During a fierce winter storm in November of 1965, winds gusting to 85 mph crumble a 375-foot cooling tower at the Ferrybridge electric generating station in northern England.

A lone snowplow struggles in vain with a 24-inch snowfall and 50-mph winds as pedestrians flounder along a Chicago street during a 1968 blizzard that paralyzed the city for several days.

Their ships sinking in the maelstrom of the English Channel, desperate sailors try to stay afloat in the worst gale in England's history. Striking with hurricane force in November 1703, the storm killed 8,000 people and destroyed 14,000 homes.

Their hats and umbrellas whipped away by 70-mph gusts, New Yorkers in this contemporary newspaper engraving fight for their footing in the blizzard of 1888. Striking in March after an unusually mild winter, the storm left 400 dead.

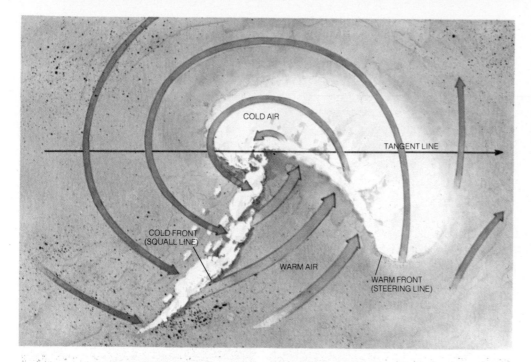

COLD AIR

TANGENT LINE

COLD FRONT
(SQUALL LINE)

WARM AIR

WARM FRONT
(STEERING LINE)

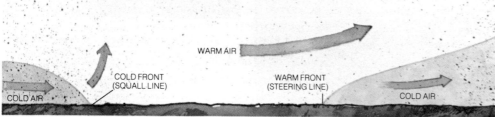

WARM AIR

COLD FRONT
(SQUALL LINE)

WARM FRONT
(STEERING LINE)

COLD AIR

COLD AIR

Developed in 1918 by the pioneers at Norway's Bergen school, this sickle-shaped model of a cyclonic storm system was a major breakthrough in meteorology. The cyclone is born when a ripple of warm air plunges into cold air and corkscrews counterclockwise around a low-pressure center. Precipitation results along two frontal zones as moisture-laden warm air is lifted over the cold air. The storm system as a whole (*shown in cross section at bottom*) moves along the tangent line.

An American meteorologist named Jerome Namias remembered early forecasts at the United States Weather Bureau as exercises in "isobaric geometry." After receiving the all-important pressure map, the forecaster would consult any number of separate maps that detailed the distribution of clouds, precipitation, temperatures and wind. Then he would attempt to predict where the low pressure was going to move, using "hundreds of rules," derived from previous behavior of storm tracks, that Namias said he "tried to memorize in order to learn how to forecast. There were confusing and seemingly contradictory rules involving pressure changes, etcetera, and I soon had to give up since my mind didn't have enough storage."

Bjerknes and his Norwegian colleagues were determined to substitute for these haphazard rules a foundation of science that could support the making of practical day-to-day forecasts. His first concern, as in 1904, was to determine the present state of the atmosphere, and to do that he needed infinitely more information than was available. In all of Norway, there were only 14 meteorological observation stations—enough perhaps for broad generalizations about the approaching weather, but not nearly enough for Bjerknes' purposes.

With spring planting only weeks away, Bjerknes moved swiftly to reorganize Norway's weather service. In Bergen his son Jacob took charge of forecasting for the western region, and another assistant, Halvor Solberg, went to the capital to tend to the eastern areas. From the beginning, Bjerknes was aware of a major difficulty that threatened the entire project. Weather reports from Britain and Iceland, both located to the west of Norway, were now regarded as military secrets and were no longer provided. Because all the low-pressure areas that crossed Norway came from the west, the absence of information from that area eliminated advance warning of approaching bad weather.

But the elder Bjerknes had encountered the same problem once before, when the German Army in France was forced to do without any observation of the weather coming from the hostile west. The military forecasters had been able to

function by greatly increasing the frequency and density of their observations. Three sets of readings each day, taken at the surface and aloft, had been communicated by field telephone and by telegraph to district headquarters, where detailed local forecasts were made. Bjerknes proposed to employ the same method in Norway, and in this he found an unexpected wartime ally.

Zealously guarding the nation's neutrality, the Norwegian Navy had established sentry stations along the western coast to watch for incursions by German submarines. Most of the observers were seasoned sailors, and Bjerknes immediately recruited 10 of them for twice-daily weather observations. In addition he signed up fishermen, lighthouse keepers and farmers until by the beginning of the summer forecast season he was receiving data from approximately 75 stations in western Norway. Once this information was coordinated in Bergen, it gave the clearest picture yet of the workings of the weather.

It quickly became apparent that the cyclone, or low-pressure storm system, was far more complex than anyone had realized. Forecasters had for decades assumed that precipitation surrounded the center of low pressure. But after only a few months of studying the summer cyclones that passed across Norway, Jacob Bjerknes published a paper that demolished the old ideas.

He explained that the precipitation pattern of the cyclone never exhibited the neat circular configuration long attributed to it, but rather looked most often like a thick-bladed sickle. From the center of an eastward-traveling low, the sickle blade would curve to the southeast, its handle to the southwest. The inward, or cutting, edge of the sickle blade Jacob called the steering line, and the forward edge of the handle he named the squall line. A broad band of precipitation extended in front of the steering line and a narrow, more violent one behind the squall line; between the two lines a tongue of noticeably warmer air extended up into the center of the low-pressure system.

An observer located to the south of the center of such a system as it moved east would first experience a progressively thicker overcast. Then, there would be a period of rain followed by a sudden increase in temperature; as the temperature rose, the rain would cease and the skies might even clear briefly. Finally, there would be a short period of violent showers, a drop in temperature and a return to clear, cool weather as the cyclone finally moved on.

As complicated as it was, the new scenario soon proved to be an oversimplification; the profile seldom fit any existing cyclone exactly. But it was nevertheless extremely useful. Not only did it permit far more accurate predictions of the precipitation patterns that could be expected from a storm, but it yielded an unmistakable signal of the storm's intentions. For the analysts soon noticed that a line drawn tangent to the curve of the steering line where it met the squall line in the center of the low indicated the cyclone's eastbound course. How long the storm would travel in that direction was a separate question, but the indicator was far more accurate than any deductions made from changes in the barometric pressure over a wide area in the general direction of advance.

The utility of the new cyclone model was soon apparent; by using it in his predictions, Jacob Bjerknes cut his percentage of error in half between July and September. No one could say whether the improvement materially affected that year's agricultural production, and the Bergen school claimed no breakthroughs—"no brilliant results," Vilhelm Bjerknes would say of that first summer's work—but there was one startling discovery with immediate significance. And it was only the beginning.

The armistice in November 1918 did not end the demands on Norwegian meteorology. Food prices were still exorbitant and the need for improved agricultural forecasting was unabated. Furthermore, a national enthusiasm for commercial aviation added to the demand for precise prediction of conditions aloft as well as at the surface. Vilhelm Bjerknes was not only willing but eager to continue; the results of the first summer had more than overcome his reluctance to partici-

pate in "practical" meteorology. "It is especially desirable," he now said, "to be able to establish as intimate a cooperation as possible between the theoretical dynamic meteorology and the practical weather forecasting system."

Early in 1919, Bjerknes merged the forecasting project with the Bergen Museum's Geophysical Institute, and moved everything into a large frame house on the edge of Bergen's central park. The Bjerknes family lived on the ground floor while the scientists and forecasters toiled at long wooden tables in the large upstairs rooms. The environment was relaxed and homelike—the formidable Professor Bjerknes often carried wood to the stoves to keep his assistants warm as they worked—and the progress it engendered was dazzling.

Studying Jacob Bjerknes' new cyclone model, the Bergen meteorologists soon realized that the patterns of precipitation in a storm were not dictated merely by the lowering of barometric pressure. And the more they puzzled over what did cause precipitation, the more important that tongue of warm air intruding into the low, surrounded on three sides by cold air, seemed to be. It gradually dawned

At Norway's Bergen school of meteorology, housed in the upstairs rooms of Vilhelm Bjerknes' home, two of the institution's leading scientists—Tor Bergeron (*center*) and Jacob Bjerknes, Vilhelm's son (*right*)—analyze weather data while the woman at left records the information on maps.

In this remarkable aerial photograph, a warm, cloudy air mass can be seen sloping gently upward over the top of a colder air mass near Stony Stratford, England. As the warm front moves forward, it pushes the cold air into a wedge shape; rain falls from the clouds near the point of the wedge, where the warm air, cooling and expanding as it rises, loses its capacity to retain moisture.

on Vilhelm Bjerknes that "the weather changes because the masses of air move, and change their internal state."

Not pressure fields, but masses of air—it was a fateful change in concept. For if there were discrete masses of air, defined by characteristics including not only barometric pressure but also temperature, humidity, wind velocity, cloud cover, etc., then it followed that these masses had boundaries. Viewed from this angle, the steering line and squall line of Jacob's cyclone model took on a new significance; they defined a boundary, a sharp discontinuity between two masses of air.

By the end of 1919, when he wrote his annual report for the Carnegie Institution, Vilhelm Bjerknes offered a fundamentally new explanation for the mechanics of weather: "The atmosphere is crossed and recrossed by surfaces of discontinuity, separating from each other masses of air having more or less different velocity and different physical properties. Almost every change of weather is due to the passage of a surface of this kind."

The essence of the cyclone, wrote Bjerknes, was not its low pressure, but the discontinuity between the tongue of warm air that protruded into its center and the colder air to the north. Along the eastern boundary of the advancing warm air—the steering line of Jacob Bjerknes' model—the warmer air was flowing upward over the denser cold air. As it rose, it cooled; the water vapor it carried

condensed into clouds that soon began to release precipitation. Along the western boundary of the warm air mass the colder air was nosing under the warm air and lifting it so rapidly that the precipitation was more violent—often in the form of thunderstorms.

This three-dimensional concept of the structure of the cyclonic storm meant a fundamental change in forecasting procedures. "It will be of high importance," wrote Vilhelm Bjerknes, "to arrange the observations so that the formation of the discontinuities can be detected at an early state, and their propagation followed as accurately as possible." Another ramification of the Bergen school discoveries was something of an irony: Amid all the theoretical physics, Bjerknes introduced to modern meteorology the practice of simply watching the sky.

The idea that certain kinds of clouds presaged storms had been persistent in folklore at least since the time of Aristotle. But it had never gained much currency among serious scientists. Intent on charting their pressure fields, meteorologists had been interested only in the broad patterns of any overcast. But the new, three-dimensional concept of the cyclone and its processes implied that different types of clouds would be formed by the different processes. In fact, the cloud forms signal the processes with surprising consistency. Wrote Bjerknes: "The appearance of the sky in the different parts of the cyclone is so characteristic, and

CUMULONIMBUS

develops in so typical a way during the passage of the whole system, that it will always be recognized when one has become acquainted with it."

An observer to the southeast of an approaching cyclone that corresponded to Jacob Bjerknes' model would first see high, thin cirrus clouds that would thicken gradually from wisps to a "milky veil." As the steering line approached, the clouds would become progressively lower and thicker, of a type known as stratus. Eventually, the stratus would turn to dark, heavy nimbostratus, and there would be a period of steady rain. It would then clear gradually. Soon, however, a line of billowy cumulus clouds followed closely by cumulonimbus, or thunderstorm, clouds would announce the approach of the squall line with its brief but heavy showers. Vilhelm Bjerknes soon had his network of weather observers reporting regularly on the type and altitude of the clouds they could see, and the practice became central to the new meteorology.

The advances of the Bergen school had by now assumed something of a pattern. After a busy period of collecting and analyzing large volumes of information and fashioning daily forecasts, the scientists would find time to reflect on the broader meaning of the data, particularly as it affected their earlier, mathematical theories about the atmosphere. Once again, in the winter of 1919, this symbiosis between fact and theory produced stunning results.

Several factors had combined in 1919 to increase the volume of data. The daily forecasting project, which originally had operated only during the summer growing season, was extended into the autumn and winter, when storms were much more frequent. And the forecasters decided to request a third daily set of observations relating to the cyclonic rain and wind patterns. In addition, with the end of the War, important weather observations were once again available from Great Britain and Iceland to the west.

During the autumn, Halvor Solberg, who was still in charge of forecasting for the eastern section of the country, spotted a connection between two successive cyclonic storms. The squall line trailing from the first cyclone seemed to stall, bend, develop a fresh steering line in front of it and turn into a second cyclone. The researchers focused on this new concept during the late autumn, and when Vilhelm Bjerknes returned from a month of conferences abroad they presented their conclusion: Cyclones were not isolated events; they were somehow linked, and there was a pattern to their development and movement. According to

This drawing illustrates the cloud formations that often accompany the eastward movement of a frontal cyclone. An observer to the east, or right, of the storm system would see a progression of clouds beginning with high, wispy cirrus signaling the approach of the warm front (diagram). The wisps soon spread into a translucent cirrostratus veil, followed by a thickening blanket of stratus clouds that produces prolonged precipitation. After a period of partial clearing, the approaching cold front pushes the warm air mass sharply upward, building towering cumulonimbus clouds that can bring thunderstorms. Fair weather returns with the passage of the cold front.

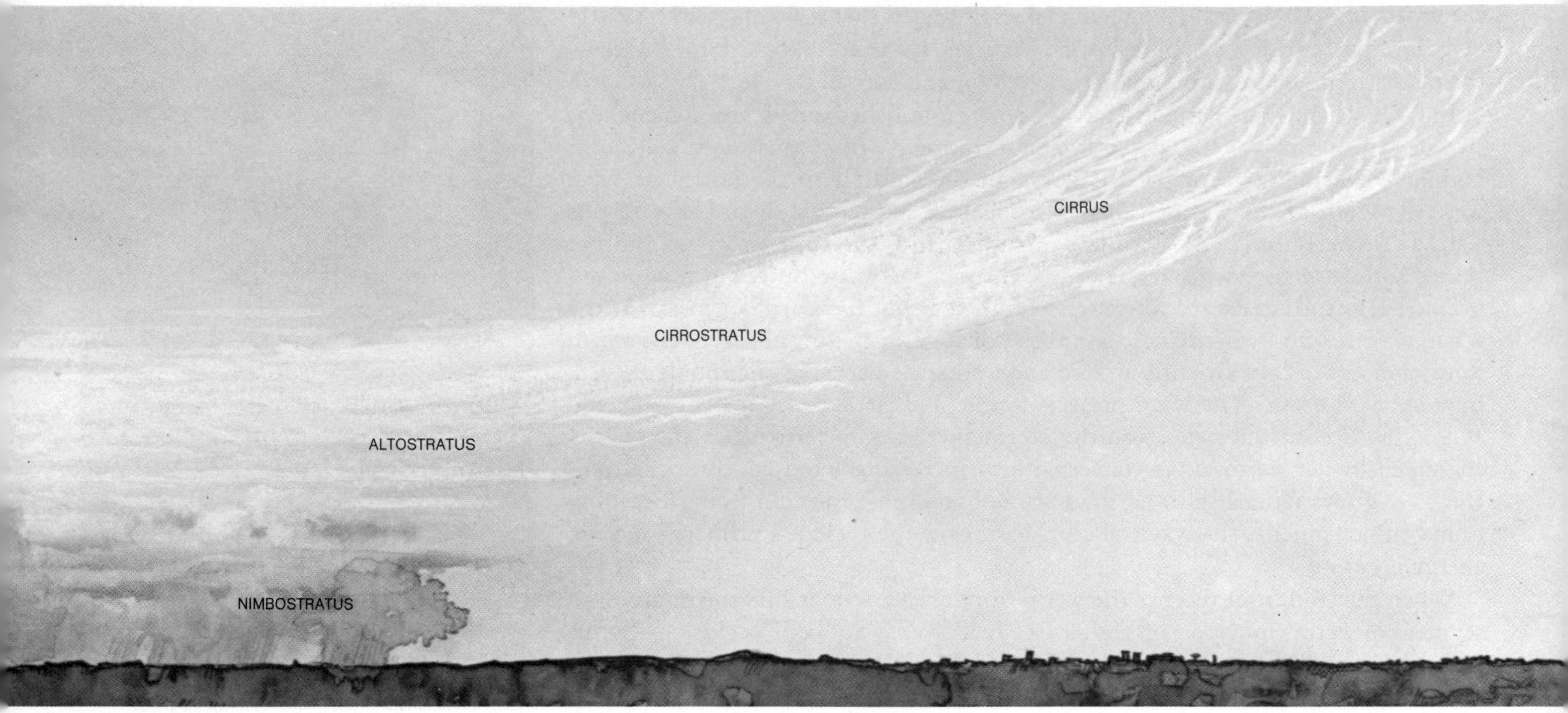

CIRRUS

CIRROSTRATUS

ALTOSTRATUS

NIMBOSTRATUS

Robert Marc Friedman, an American meteorologist who became a fervent researcher and historian of the Bergen school's achievements, the next crucial step was taken at a round-table discussion in mid-December. It was then that the Bergen scientists expanded their germinal idea to its full, electrifying potential. Within six months they had confirmed a monumental new theory of storms.

In July of 1920, Vilhelm Bjerknes began his annual report to the Carnegie Institution with a reference to the previous year's emphasis on the cyclone's surfaces of discontinuity. He went on to say that these were not just the steering and squall lines of individual cyclones, but part of a longer line of discontinuity, along which the cyclones "follow each other like pearls on a string." It was now evident, continued Bjerknes, that successive lines of discontinuity "are seen from day to day to sweep over the chart as curves of a more or less wavy form." He had realized that what showed up on the limited scope of local weather maps as successive lines were in fact only segments that were joined beyond the boundaries of the map in what he now called "a single continuous line of wavy forms" encircling the entire Northern Hemisphere. "From the polar regions heavy cold air tends to flow out along the ground, being separated from the overlying warmer air by a surface of discontinuity—a kind of 'polar front.' "

The term front had been borrowed from the combat terminology of World War I, and it seemed particularly apt to describe the conflict between cold and warm air masses along the wavy line of discontinuity. The polar air was characterized as the enemy, attacking toward the Equator, while the warm southern air counterattacked toward the Pole. Cyclonic storms were the most intense battles in this atmospheric global war. "The warm air is victorious to the east of the center," in the warm salient that projected into the low-pressure area, wrote Bjerknes. "Here it rises up over the cold, and approaches in this way its goal, the Pole. The cold air, which is pressed hard, escapes to the west, in order suddenly to make a sharp turn toward the south, and attacks the warm air in the flank: it penetrates under it as a cold west wind." The steering line marked the discontinuity at the surface, where the advancing warm air rose upward over the cold air; the Bergen scientists would classify it as a warm front. The leading edge of the counterattacking cold air, surging under the warm tongue along the squall line, would now be seen as a cold front.

In the context of this hemispheric sweep of events, the Bergen scientists re-examined Jacob Bjerknes' cyclone model and realized that it was not the final and definitive portrait of a cyclonic storm. Though it was accurate as far as it went, the model represented only one stage in a long and complex cycle.

In 1922 Jacob Bjerknes and Halvor Solberg published a new and comprehensive description of the life of the cyclonic storm. At first, they said, a straight boundary exists between the east winds of the cold air to the north, and the westerly winds of the warmer air to the south. The cyclonic disturbance begins with a northerly bulge of warm air intruding into the cold air mass, and the center of the cyclone forms at the northern tip of the warm bulge, or tongue.

The bulge rolls eastward like a wave on the edge of the warm air mass. As the warm air rises up over the cold air ahead of it, rain begins ahead of the warm front, and as the cold air curls around and under the backside of the bulge, cold-front showers occur. The wave projects farther and farther into the cold air, and as long as it continues to do so the storm increases in ferocity as the energy contained in the warm air is converted into increasing wind and precipitation. But as it grows taller it also narrows at the base, until the cold front, attacking from behind, pinches the wave off at its base; now the cyclone's primary source of energy is cut off.

When the cold front reaches the warm front ahead of it, it lifts the interposing segment of warm, moist air off the surface in a process dubbed "occlusion" by the Bergen school. The front is thus virtually obliterated at the surface, although the remaining warm air aloft continues for a time to be lifted and cooled, producing precipitation. But with no further injections of warm circulation the cyclone soon dissipates.

Often, however, the trailing edge of the cold front will hook around a new wave of warm air to form a secondary cyclone that then follows, slightly to the south and east, the path of the first. Far from being isolated events, it was now apparent, cyclones often come in closely connected families in a progression for which every forecaster should be alert.

The polar-front theory of meteorology with its associated cyclone models provided well-defined three-dimensional concepts that were enormously useful. Not only did they permit better forecasts of events within cyclones, but they soon exhibited a significant long-term pattern. There proved to be a surprising regularity in the arrival of cyclone families associated with the passing of the polar front—the interval between them averaged five and a half days. Armed with this knowledge, in 1922 the Norwegian Weather Service began to issue five-day forecasts, an audacious undertaking for the time. "As the movements of the cyclone families are far more regular than those of individual cyclones," wrote Vilhelm Bjerknes, "these forecasts succeed rather better than the short-range forecasts for the next day."

But the more the new concepts were studied, the more perplexing challenges arose. The very existence of a polar front encircling the hemisphere had been postulated as a logical extension of what was observed in and near Norway. However, later measurements did not always confirm its existence. What is more, while the frontal theories accounted for most of the storm activity affecting Norway, they did not account for all of it. Practical meteorologists could not ignore the frequent thunderstorm and shower activity that took place far from any front.

It was in pursuing these loose ends that the Bergen scientists, led by a brilliant young meteorologist named Tor Bergeron, realized that not only the cyclone, but the air masses around it, had definite cycles. When Vilhelm Bjerknes had begun his quest, he had thought of the atmosphere as one enveloping mass to be studied as a unit. Then it became clear that in each hemisphere there were two significantly different air masses—one warm, one cold—separated by the polar front that circled the globe in a wavy line. Now Bergeron reached another conclusion that would be fundamental to the increasingly transformed science of

Meteorologist Halvor Solberg, seen here in a 1937 photograph, was the first to realize that cyclonic storms are interrelated. In 1920, Solberg saw that a succession of storms moved around the earth along a wavelike border, which separated polar and equatorial air masses. This border, he wrote, "marks the front battle-line between two bodies of air, and that is why it has such a contorted course, since now the warm and then the cold has dominance over the other."

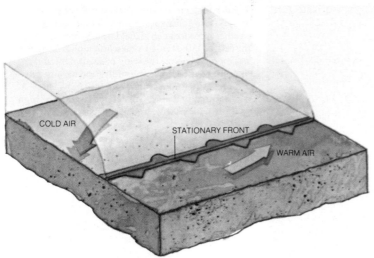

A cyclonic storm's life cycle begins along a front. In the sequence illustrated here, a stationary front has formed as cold air blocks warm air that is moving up from the south.

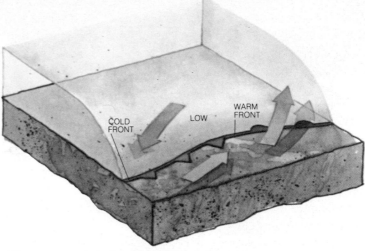

Given a counterclockwise spin by the Coriolis effect, the two conflicting air masses—delineated by warm and cold fronts—begin to rotate around a deepening low-pressure area.

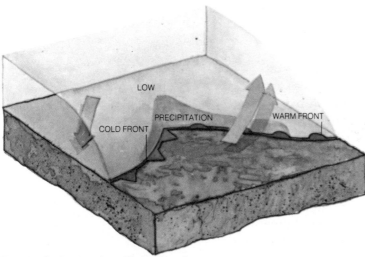

Pressing farther into the cold air mass, the moisture-laden warm air cools as it rises, causing precipitation. Meanwhile, the cold front begins to outflank the invading warm air.

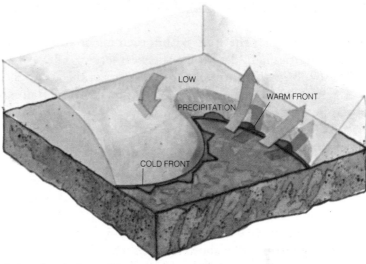

Rain and cyclonic winds increase as the cold front compresses the intrusion of warm air. Precipitation now extends farther along both fronts, though the cold-front winds are more violent.

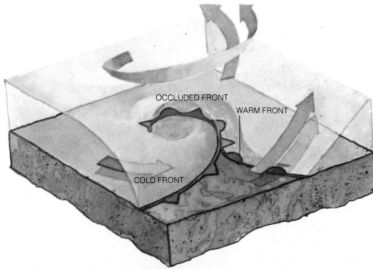

Cut off from its source by the cold front, the warm air mass lifts off the ground to form an occluded front—one that exists aloft but not at the surface. Precipitation continues from high altitude.

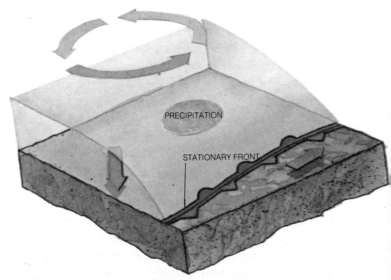

Completely isolated, the warm front disappears; the warm air sheds the last of its moisture and the storm abates. The stationary front reforms, and awaits a renewal of the storm cycle.

meteorology—that there are within each major air mass many smaller air masses whose activities help determine the weather.

These subsidiary air masses are segments of the atmosphere that remain at rest over a portion of the globe long enough to assume certain uniform characteristics of temperature and moisture. When such an air mass is set in motion by the circulation of the atmosphere, its structure and characteristics are changed by the circumstances it encounters. A polar air mass originating over northern Canada starts out cold and dry; if it moves southeasterly over land it warms near the surface and becomes vertically unstable—that is, the warmer surface air tends to rise rapidly. So long as the air mass is relatively dry, only slight cloudiness and little or no precipitation results. But should the air mass travel over water, picking up moisture as well as heat, the rising, unstable air can soon create heavy clouds and possibly rain showers, even when it is not associated with a front. The travels of the air mass determine its developing physical characteristics and the weather it produces on the way.

With this knowledge the Bergen theorists could explain why it was sometimes impossible to discern a polar front at the surface where, according to their calculations, there had to be one. The increasing warmth of an air mass moving southward over the earth could obliterate the temperature differential at the surface—but, as the scientists soon discovered, readings aloft showed the necessary temperature swing and confirmed the presence of a front.

In addition, the Bergen school offered the first clear explanation of why inclement weather arises along some fronts and not others. If the front marks the edges of two air masses with similar life histories—corresponding lengths of time over comparable surfaces—then the discontinuities between them are slight and the possibility of the formation of a cyclonic storm on their boundaries is reduced. It is when the differences in temperature and humidity are extreme that families of cyclones can be expected. Tor Bergeron arrived at four classifications of air masses that proved enduringly useful in making forecasts: Air masses that originate over land are continental, over water, maritime; those from the frigid north are polar, those from warmer latitudes, tropical. It was now obvious to the Bergen group that the standard practice of intently charting the progress of lows while remaining largely indifferent to highs was inadequate; it was the nature of the highs that determined the severity of the cyclones.

As early as 1920, Vilhelm Bjerknes began working to export the Bergen school's approach to forecasting. He envisioned a circumpolar weather service involving all the nations of the temperate latitudes, each contributing information and benefiting from ever more accurate predictions. Scientists from seven nations attended a series of conferences in Norway, and Bjerknes and his assistants—he called them his "apostles"—followed up with letters and personal visits urging foreign meteorologists to join the Bergen school on the new frontier of meteorology. "Besides making the forecast for the next day much more correct and detailed," wrote Jacob Bjerknes, "they also make very probable that forecasts for several days or perhaps weeks might be attained." And the Norwegians were able to make good on their promises; when the British finally got around to testing the new methods in the mid-1930s, said Jacob, "they were astonished over what can be obtained." But the response from other countries was slow, and almost two decades passed between the revolutionary breakthroughs of the Bergen group and their general acceptance.

The Bergen school's remarkable series of discoveries came to an end in the mid-1920s. In 1926 Vilhelm Bjerknes returned to the University of Oslo and his original profession—teaching physics. He continued to do some work in meteorology with Halvor Solberg, who joined him in Oslo, but increasingly turned his attention to theoretical physics. When he died in 1951 he was working on the completion of a theory originated by his father. Work at the Bergen Geophysical Institute continued, of course; Jacob Bjerknes remained there for more than 10 years after his father's return to Oslo. Then, in 1940, while Jacob was on a brief visit to the United States, Norway was invaded and occupied by Germany. Unable to return home, the younger Bjerknes took a position as professor of meteorology at the University of California; there he continued his research until his death in 1975.

After the leading lights of the Bergen school began to disperse in 1926, however, other scientists rose to prominence, refining the Bergen theories and building on them as meteorology and the study of storms became an increasingly mature science.

Chief among these inheritors of Vilhelm Bjerknes' mantle was Carl-Gustaf Rossby, a brilliant Swedish researcher who himself had studied briefly with the Bergen school. In 1926 Rossby won a fellowship for a year of work with the U.S. Weather Bureau in Washington, D.C. The 28-year-old Rossby arrived in the United States as determined to spread the gospel of air-mass analysis and frontal systems as the most fervent of the Bergen school's apostles. But the complex new theories at first fell on deaf ears, and it took Rossby more than a decade of missionary work—a year at the weather bureau plus 10 years as a professor at the Massachusetts Institute of Technology—before American meteorologists finally began using Bergen methods in their forecasting. Were he a vengeful man, Rossby might have made much of the fact that there were no frontal systems drawn on the official forecast maps at the time of the terrible 1938 hurricane— but fronts and cyclones were prominently displayed on the maps drawn to explain that unforeseen disaster.

The victory was certified in 1939 when Rossby was appointed assistant chief of the U.S. Weather Bureau in charge of research and education. But Rossby's great achievement was not so much in bringing American meteorology into the modern era; his most important gift was a momentous breakthrough in research that added a whole new dimension to the science.

For a number of years Rossby had been studying the nature of the polar front's "more or less wavy form," as Vilhelm Bjerknes had described it in 1920. Rossby became interested in the winds aloft—especially the great curving sweeps of the westerlies that race along high over the edges of the polar air masses. He found that these winds aloft define a series of lobes—usually four to six—extending into the warmer southern air, and that the lobes generally proceed in an eastward direction. The curving boundaries of these lobes correspond almost exactly to the surface fronts along which families of cyclones are arrayed, in the elder Bjerknes'

Long ribbons of cirrus clouds mark the passage of the polar jet stream, a narrow band of high-velocity wind that girdles the Northern Hemisphere at an altitude of around 30,000 feet. When this photo was taken in April 1956, the polar jet was racing over Kansas City, Missouri, at 200 mph—intensifying cyclonic activity at the earth's surface and sharply increasing the chance of severe thunderstorms and tornadoes.

words, "like pearls on a string." It seemed evident that the high-altitude winds had a profound effect on the cyclonic storms beneath them, but Rossby did not know how, or why.

During 1939 and 1940, Rossby completed a dynamic theory that explained the actions of the high-altitude westerlies in terms of the effect of the earth's rotation on existing currents in the atmosphere. Equatorial air moving northward, he said, tends to spin cyclonically, or counterclockwise, while polar air moving south increasingly tends to turn anticyclonically. The result is Bjerknes' "wavy line" of demarcation, meandering across the temperate latitudes between the extremities of the warm and cold air masses. This line—the polar front— delineates a pattern of lobes that soon came to be known as long, or Rossby, waves. In what became famous as the "dish-pan" experiment, Rossby was later able to duplicate the shape and behavior of these long waves in a spinning pan of water whose edges were being warmed while the center was being cooled. And he devised a relatively simple formula that could predict the speed of the winds aloft along the polar front.

It was Rossby's research that explained what some astonished World War II pilots discovered at altitudes of around 30,000 feet—ribbons of westerly winds coursing through the temperate latitudes at upward of 200 miles per hour. Aircraft accidentally flying with such winds behind them arrived in England, for example, hours ahead of time while those flying against these winds could come to a virtual standstill. Rossby's theories showed that the dynamics of the conflicting air masses produce a core of these high-velocity winds directly over polar fronts along the line of strongest pressure and temperature discontinuities.

The meanderings of this jet stream, as it was soon called, strongly affect the course of cyclonic storms, and its velocity is directly related to the strength of the storms that form under it; the faster the jet stream over a cyclone, the more air whisked away, and the more intense the storm.

At last it was even possible to explain why cyclones always form under the Rossby wave's leading edge—on the section of the polar front that stretches from the southernmost extremity of a lobe of polar air northeastward to the northernmost advance of the equatorial air. As the jet stream curves around the southern

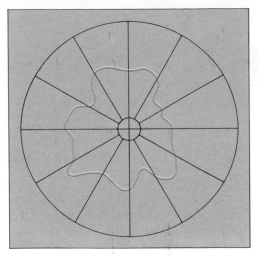

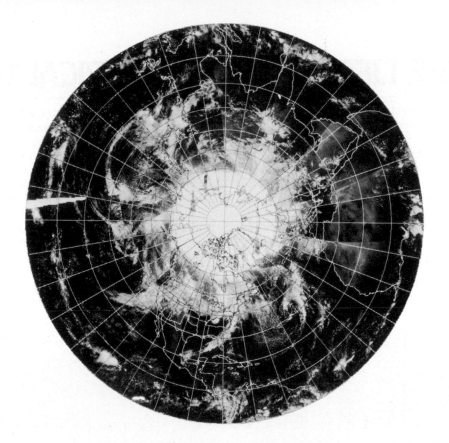

A satellite view of the Northern Hemisphere (*right*) shows the cloud patterns of January 4, 1982; the arcs of clouds that pinwheel toward the center of the image are associated with frontal cyclones. The diagram above traces the circuitous path of the polar jet stream on the day the image was made. A comparison of the photograph and the diagram illustrates a direct relationship between the jet stream's high-velocity winds and the frontal cyclones beneath them.

end of the lobe of polar air, it is turning counterclockwise, and imparting a cyclonic spin to the upper air. Any cyclonic disturbance below it is thus encouraged and intensified. At the northern end of a long wave, however, in turning southward the upper air wheels clockwise, thus slowing down and stopping any cyclonic disturbance under it.

The indefatigable Rossby returned to Sweden in 1950 to explore a whole new universe of complexities in the study of atmospheric chemistry: He envisioned a biochemical balance among all the elements present in the air, the seas and the earth that was as vast and as significant as the thermodynamic balance he had spent his life studying.

In the United States after his departure, the swift advance of technology offered meteorologists an ever-increasing array of sophisticated tools: long-range radar, space satellites, high-speed computers. Yet on every weather map, in every textbook and in the minds of every analyst, forecaster and researcher concerned with the temperate latitudes of the world, the fronts, cyclone models and air-mass concepts of the Bergen school remained indispensable. Their presence provided an eloquent answer to a contemptuous question about the Bergen school posed in the 1920s by a German meteorologist: "How could anything important scientifically come out of tiny conservative Norway?" **Ω**

THE LIFE CYCLE OF A TROPICAL TERROR

Tropical cyclones are neither as large as frontal storms nor as violent as tornadoes, but they possess one unqualified distinction: They are the deadliest storms on earth. Each year they snuff out more lives worldwide than all other storms combined.

These cyclones are born in the steamy late-summer environment of the tropics (*below*). As the sun warms the oceans, evaporation and conduction transfer heat to the atmosphere so rapidly that air and water temperatures seldom differ by more than 2° F. The water vapor generated by such evaporation is the fuel that drives a tropical storm, because as the vapor condenses into clouds and precipitation it pumps enormous amounts of heat into the cyclone. The fuel supply is controlled by the evaporation rate—which explains why cyclones cannot develop when the ocean temperature is below about 76° F.

The frequent product of this mix of heat and moisture is an aggregation of thunderstorms that can become the seedling for a tropical cyclone—but it must be nurtured further. The trigger for most Atlantic hurricanes is an easterly wave (*opposite, top*), a westward-migrating low-pressure center that may have begun as an African thunderstorm. Typhoons in the Pacific and Indian Oceans, and a few hurricanes in the Atlantic, emerge from waves in the equatorial trough, the calm, cloudy doldrums that separate the trade winds of the two hemispheres (*opposite, bottom*).

The seedlings face a hostile, capricious environment and a problematical future. Only a handful—perhaps nine of the more than 100 seedlings tracked each year in the Atlantic, for example—survive to become gale-force tropical storms or full-fledged hurricanes.

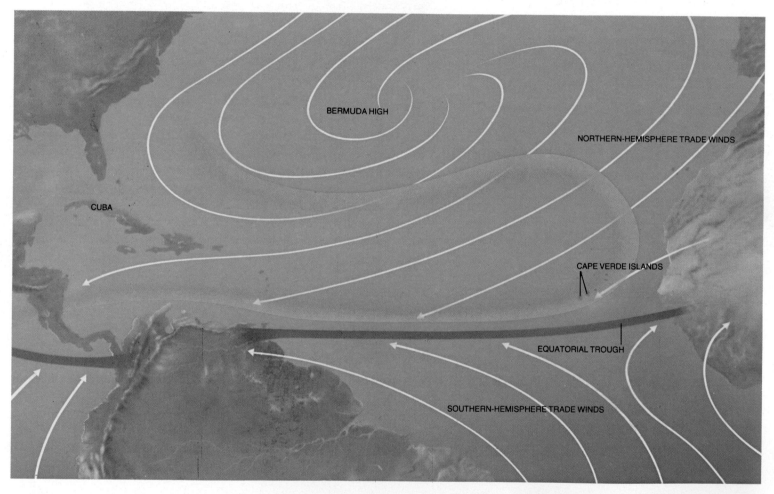

The dimensions of the breeding grounds for tropical cyclones (*purple*), shown above for a typical September in the Atlantic, vary constantly in each of the world's oceans. The northern boundary reflects an ocean temperature of 76° F.; the southern boundary is about 60 miles north of the equatorial trough (*red line*), the zone where the trade winds converge. Within the breeding grounds (*right*), hurricanes are born only when wind velocities at different altitudes are similar; wind shear tends to pull seedling storms apart. Few storms appear in the eastern reaches of an ocean because an inversion—a shallow layer of air that gets warmer with height, the inverse of the normal situation—blocks air parcels rising from the moist low-level air. Cyclones are more likely to form farther west, where thunderstorms weaken the inversion and fill the dry middle atmosphere with moisture (*blue*).

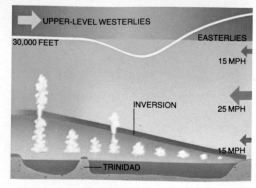

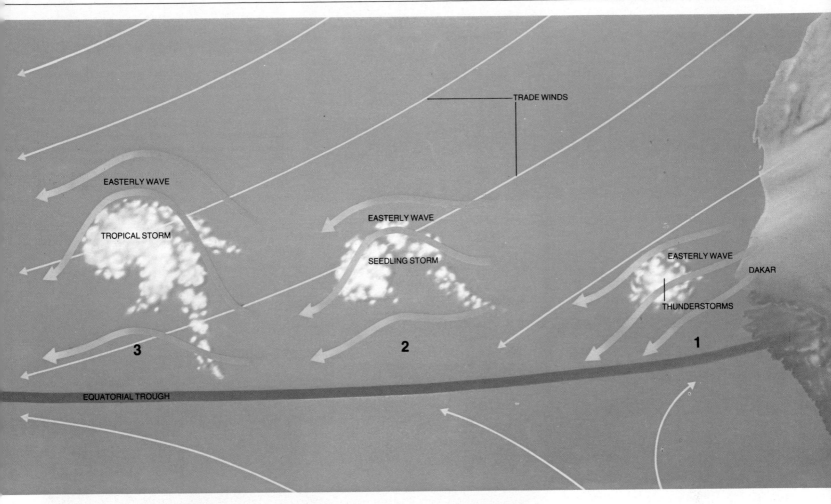

TRADE WINDS

EASTERLY WAVE

TROPICAL STORM

EASTERLY WAVE

SEEDLING STORM

EASTERLY WAVE

DAKAR

THUNDERSTORMS

3

2

1

EQUATORIAL TROUGH

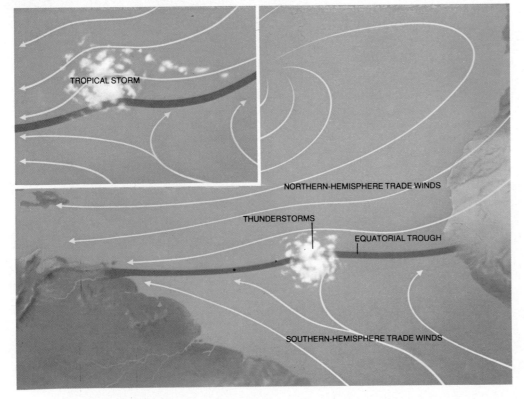

TROPICAL STORM

NORTHERN-HEMISPHERE TRADE WINDS

THUNDERSTORMS

EQUATORIAL TROUGH

SOUTHERN-HEMISPHERE TRADE WINDS

During the Atlantic hurricane season about two easterly waves per week drift westward over the Atlantic at roughly 20 mph. At first such waves barely bend the low-level winds (*purple arrows*) and produce only innocuous rain showers (*1*). But when atmospheric conditions are favorable, vigorous thunderstorms and the pumping action of high-altitude winds magnify a wave, building a cluster of severe thunderstorms (*2*) and eventually a full-fledged tropical storm (*3*).

An alternate scenario for the birth of a hurricane begins when Southern Hemisphere trade winds push a slight dent into the equatorial trough, creating a wave northward. In autumn, when the trough is located farthest from the Equator, the Coriolis effect of the earth's rotation is strong enough to start the thunderstorms in such waves spinning cyclonically. Northern Hemisphere trade winds then may undercut the wave (*inset*) and carry it off as a tropical storm while the equatorial trough re-forms behind it.

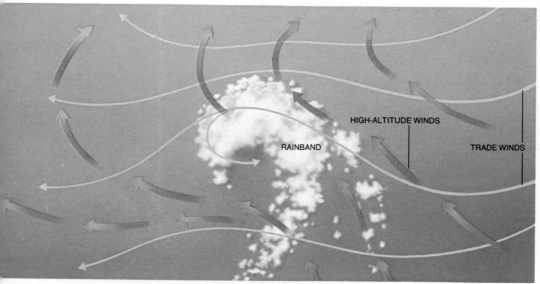

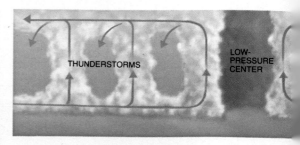

In a tropical storm, organized circulation connects and intensifies the seedling's independent thunderstorms (above): A deepening low-pressure center sucks in moist low-level air, convection lifts the air, and high pressure aloft pushes it outward. As the anvil-shaped thunderstorm tops merge over a single comma-like rainband (left), the storm's course is a compromise between two steering currents—low-level trade winds (blue arrows) blowing from the east and high-altitude winds (tan arrows) curving to the northeast.

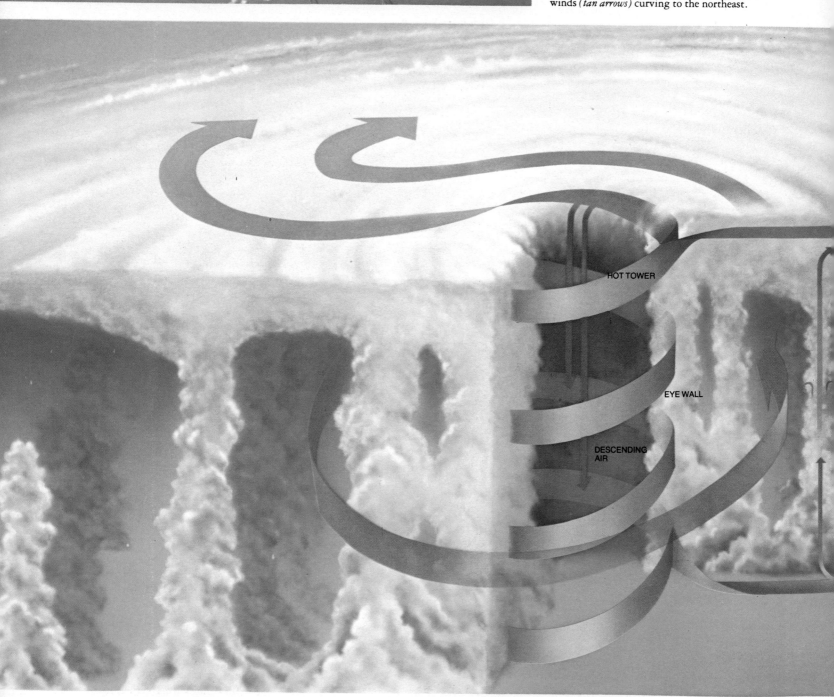

Two events 40,000 feet above the ocean can transform an ordinary hurricane into an explosive superstorm: A strong jet stream may whisk away the cyclone's exhaust, accelerating its circulation. Or a large pocket of cold air may meander near the cyclone; when cold air sinks through warmer tropical air the hurricane's exhaust rushes into the resulting void, accelerating the surface winds.

The height and vigor of a hurricane's rainbands increase steadily toward the energy-packed core of the storm, as can be seen in the cross section below. At the eye wall, air ascends through a few hot towers—isolated columns of air that soar upward at speeds of 30 or more miles an hour. On top of the storm system some of the hurricane's exhaust falls back into the eye (red arrows), but centrifugal force sends most of it spiraling counterclockwise into the outflow cloud shield. About 150 miles from the eye, a high-pressure ridge aloft becomes the main factor driving the exhaust, and the Coriolis effect gradually bends the flow into a clockwise spiral.

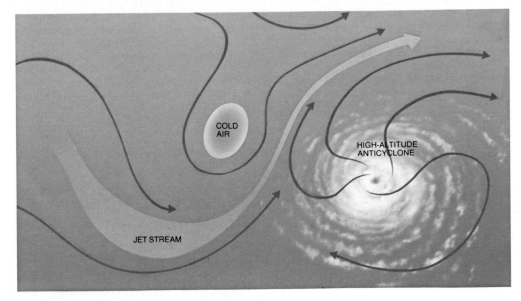

COLD AIR

HIGH-ALTITUDE ANTICYCLONE

JET STREAM

OUTFLOW CLOUD SHIELD

SPIRAL RAINBANDS

From Seedling to Cyclone

The sole difference between a harmless cluster of thunderstorms and a dangerous cyclone is the rotation that organizes weather systems. This spin, which meteorologists call vorticity, is ever-present in temperate latitudes, where the Coriolis effect of the earth's rotation is pronounced. But in the tropics the weak Coriolis effect must be augmented by the wind itself.

When two wind currents move side by side, the faster current tends to curl around the slower one. If the faster current is on the right (viewed from upwind), the curl is to the left, yielding positive vorticity in the Northern Hemisphere because it adds to the counterclockwise Coriolis effect; a right-hand curl creates negative vorticity. A curving wind also possesses vorticity—positive for a left-hand turn, negative for a right turn.

When positive vorticity becomes strong enough to spin a storm seedling, it starts a chain reaction. The thunderstorms, now revitalized by a steady influx of warm, moist air, organize around a deepening low-pressure center, called a tropical depression. This dramatically increases the likelihood of hurricane formation; fully 70 per cent of these depressions develop into hurricanes.

The depression becomes a tropical storm when its winds reach gale force, 39 miles per hour. The storm often already has as much total energy as a hurricane, but its winds are widely distributed and hence much slower; the ring of maximum wind may be as much as 200 miles across. The final step to hurricane status merely concentrates this energy. As pressure falls at the storm center, the ring of maximum wind contracts dramatically, until it is perhaps 30 miles in diameter. Outside this circle the velocity drops rapidly, but within it the fury of the hurricane reigns supreme.

As a hurricane approaches land, a gradually shelving sea floor divides the huge, wind-driven surface waves into smaller and smaller fragments far from shore *(below)*, because each wave breaks repeatedly as its subsurface portion *(dark blue)* runs aground. But the gently sloping bottom makes the storm surge itself much worse by pushing up the 300-foot-deep column of wind-churned water beneath the hurricane's eye. This column, topped by a two-foot dome of water sucked upward by the low pressure in the eye, surges perhaps 15 feet above normal sea level, submerging low-lying regions far inland. Even a bay protected by barrier islands *(right)* is not safe. Here water cannot spread sideways, so the hurricane winds heave it inland in a surge that is usually worse than the one on the open coast.

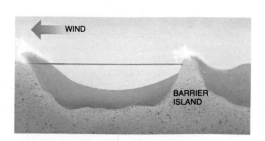

WIND

BARRIER ISLAND

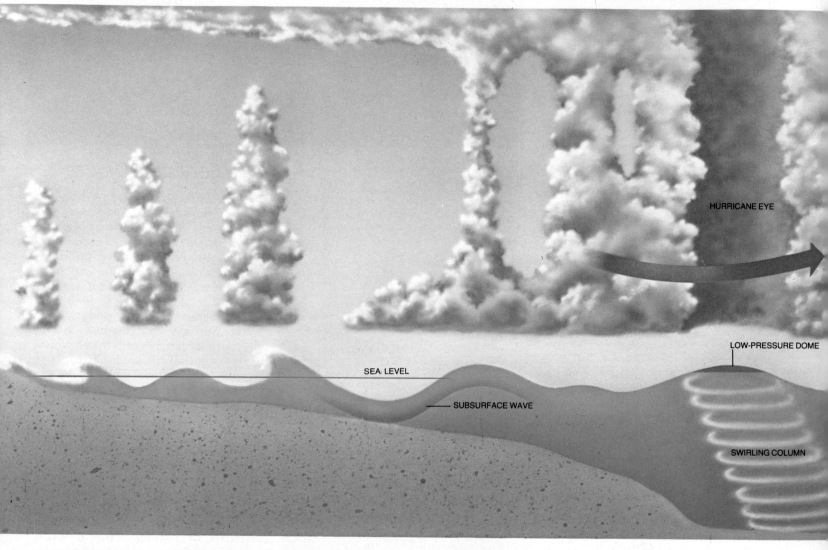

HURRICANE EYE

LOW-PRESSURE DOME

SEA LEVEL

SUBSURFACE WAVE

SWIRLING COLUMN

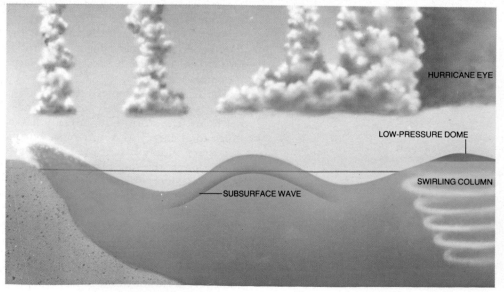

HURRICANE EYE

LOW-PRESSURE DOME

SWIRLING COLUMN

SUBSURFACE WAVE

Storm surge is less severe in deep, rapidly shelving coastal waters, such as those off Martinique and Jamaica. The waves in the hurricane's vanguard do not begin to break until they are within a mile of land, then batter the waterfront as 20-foot combers. But the swirling column beneath the eye, the most dangerous part of the surge, dissipates harmlessly against the steep ocean bottom; in all, the sea level may be raised less than three feet.

When a tropical cyclone hits land, it enters a cold, inhospitable climate where it usually dissipates rapidly. Yet the storm often takes its greatest toll during its decline.

Ninety per cent of a hurricane's victims are claimed when it first smashes ashore, not by its powerful winds but by its storm surge—the roiling mound of sea water that is the deadly companion of every tropical cyclone. The first sign of a storm surge may arrive nearly a week before the hurricane, as prevailing winds ahead of the storm begin to pile up as much as four feet of water against hundreds of miles of coastline.

When the storm is about 100 miles offshore, huge waves driven by winds in the storm's right side begin crashing ashore; the surf's roar can be heard miles inland. Then comes the most destructive compo-

nent of all, the swirling bulge of water beneath the cyclone's eye.

The surge can be exacerbated by several factors: coincidence of the storm's onset with high tide; a concave coastline that prevents the rising water from spreading sideways; a fast-moving storm that does not allow time for the water to spread; and, most of all, shallow coastal waters (opposite). The resulting surge may be more than 25 feet above normal sea level.

Tropical cyclones that curve away from land into colder waters often are considered harmless, but they too have destructive potential. Rather than dying quietly, such storms frequently evolve into particularly nasty extratropical cyclones (below) that can go on to devastate shipping and even pummel another continent.

When a tropical cyclone enters temperate latitudes and can no longer draw on a warm ocean for sustenance (inset), its winds abate, the eye quickly disappears and the storm assumes an elliptical shape. Should the moribund cyclone encounter an existing cold front, however, it can elongate and impose its circulation over a vast expanse of ocean. In this way a tropical cyclone can achieve reincarnation as a vicious extratropical cyclone whose tightly packed pressure lines reflect winds that once again exceed hurricane force.

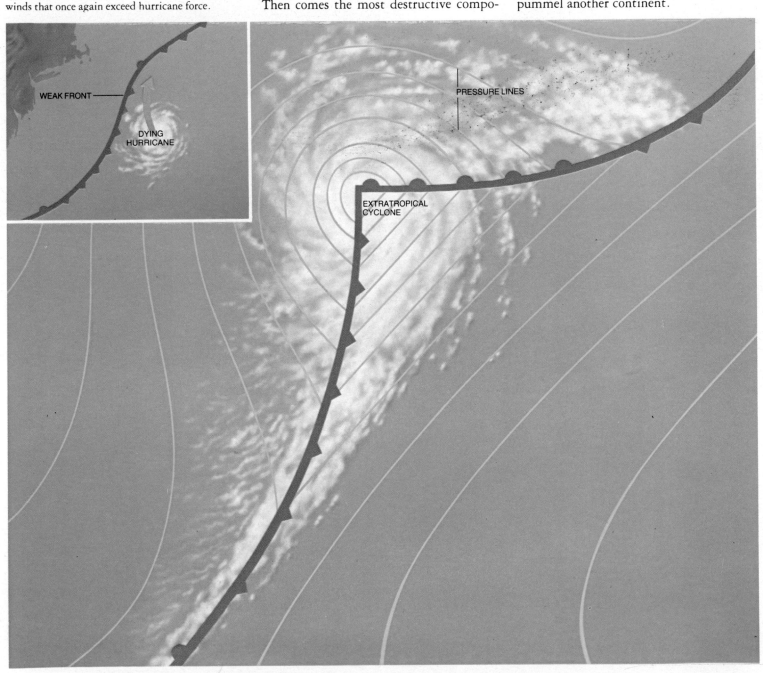

WEAK FRONT

DYING HURRICANE

PRESSURE LINES

EXTRATROPICAL CYCLONE

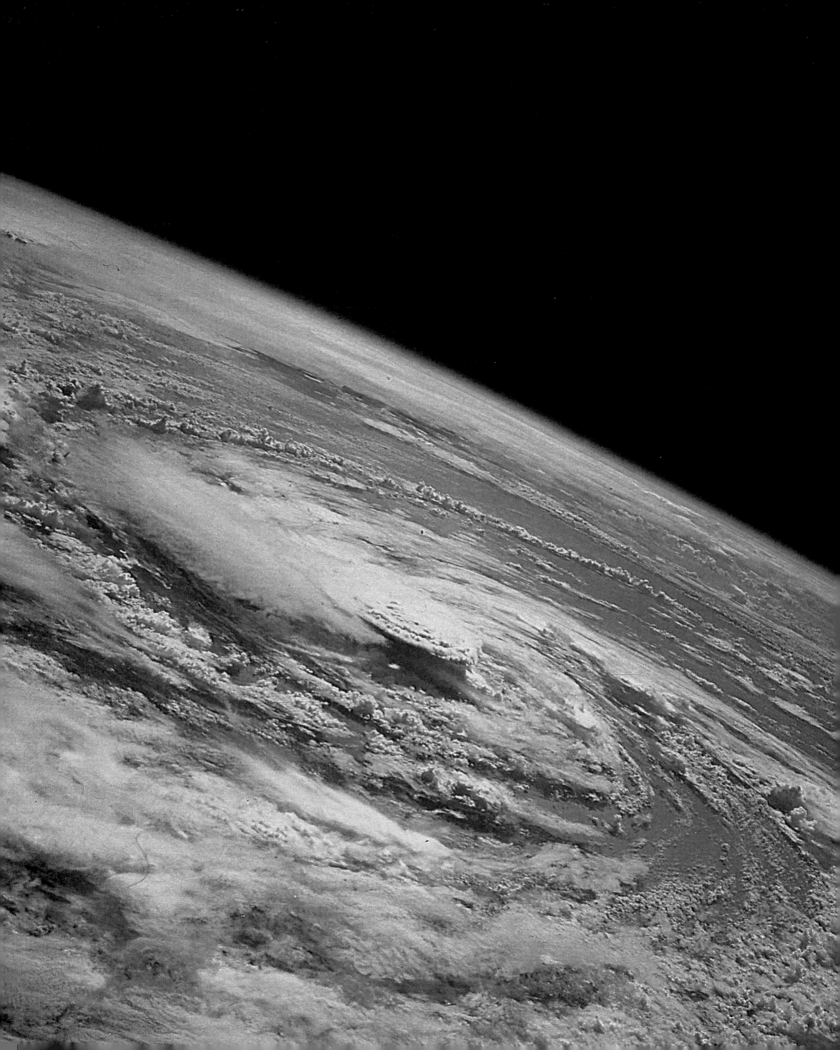

Chapter 4

HUNTING THE HURRICANE

Since the early 1900s, the pioneers of modern meteorology have performed wonders in their struggle to understand storms. Today, no tempest on earth—except possibly a freak tornado—can escape detection or come upon a helpless population completely by surprise. Nevertheless, it remains unhappily true that no forecaster can yet say with absolute certainty exactly where or when any given storm is going to strike, or precisely how severe it is going to be. And no storm has proved more frustratingly unpredictable than the tropical cyclone—called a hurricane in the Atlantic, a typhoon in the Pacific.

By the mid-20th Century, scientists had accumulated an immense body of knowledge about these great whirling storms. They knew the general location of their breeding grounds and about when to expect them. They had constructed theories that accounted, in broad terms, for the storms' workings; and they knew the directions, on the average, the storms would travel once on the rampage. But all of the averages and generalities were of only limited value in predicting exactly what a specific storm would do in the immediate future. Indeed, when it came to outguessing these monster storms, an encounter between a United States Navy war fleet and a typhoon in World War II demonstrated that a little knowledge could be a very dangerous thing.

In mid-December of 1944, a mighty U.S. armada under Admiral William F. Halsey was dispatched to the Philippine Sea to support an invasion of the Japanese-held Philippine Islands. On Sunday morning, December 17, some 90 ships of this fleet's Task Force 38 began refueling from Navy oil tankers. The wind was blowing from the northeast at up to 35 miles per hour, and the waves were high and choppy. Several ships managed after great difficulty to take on board the hoses of the plunging oil tankers—only to have the fuel lines pull loose or tear apart. One destroyer narrowly averted a collision with a tanker as the vessels labored through the heavy seas. Shortly after noon Halsey ordered the fleet to interrupt refueling and move on in search of calmer waters. It was an increasingly urgent quest—some of the destroyers were dangerously short of fuel, and the timetable for the invasion was a tight one.

On board Halsey's flagship, the battleship *New Jersey*, the meteorologist in charge was Commander George F. Kosco, a veteran of numerous operations and a student of tropical storms. Kosco analyzed the conditions and the information available to him and made his forecast. But in the Philippine Sea in 1944, information was spotty and often inaccurate. While the Navy had set up weather stations on a few of the recaptured islands, and their observations were broadcast to the fleet as often as 12 times a day, the reports covered a relatively small area. Pilots flying from the islands reported on the weather they encountered but

Whirling bands of rain-filled clouds converge on the eye of Hurricane Gladys in this photograph taken from Apollo 7 on October 18, 1968, as the storm gathers strength before crossing the Florida peninsula. Similar photos taken by orbiting satellites and radioed back to earth make it possible to find, track and study severe storms in the farthest reaches of the planet.

rarely broke radio silence to do so, and many hours passed before their observations were available. Fleet headquarters at Pearl Harbor sent out weather map analyses twice a day, but these analyses were sketchy at best and often totally useless to units operating in the far reaches of a very large and very empty ocean.

Thus Commander Kosco had to make a critical forecast based largely on what he could see and measure himself. The fact that the winds and the strongest swell were both coming from the northeast argued against the imminent arrival of a typhoon; he knew that the strongest ocean swells emanated from the right front quadrant of an advancing tropical cyclone and ran before it, while the initial winds of its spiral circulation would be directed across the swells, not along them. Kosco attributed the gale-force winds and accompanying swells to a distant storm of some sort, located perhaps 400 to 500 miles east of the fleet. He assumed that it would be following the usual storm track for that area and would be moving northwestward. Kosco was confident that when the storm—he did not call it a typhoon—encountered the cold front whose boundary lay in a northeast-southwest line directly over the fleet, the storm's track would curve to the northeast.

Briefed on Kosco's scenario, Admiral Halsey decided to set a northwest-ward course to move out of the worst weather and to interpose the cold front between the storm and the fleet. By late afternoon, the ships' barometers were rising again, the seas had moderated and Kosco's analysis seemed to have been confirmed.

Still, the evening of December 17 offered some omens that weather-wise mariners respected. A lurid sunset—"sailors' delight" in the middle latitudes, but a harbinger of foul weather in the tropics—lingered in the sky, contrasting with black, oily seas flecked with foam. After a brief moderation, the waves rose again until the smaller aircraft carriers were plunging so hard that they were in peril of taking green water over their flight decks, 60 feet above the water line.

In such ominous conditions a centuries-old dictum advised mariners in the Northern Hemisphere how to locate the center of a storm: Face the wind and the storm would be about 110 degrees to starboard. Admiral Halsey was well to the north of the Equator; had he followed the rule on the evening of December 17, with the winds out of the northeast, he would have placed the storm to the southeast of the task force. From there, the normal storm track would have led straight toward the fleet (page 95). But Halsey's weather expert was convinced that the storm was by now northeast of the fleet and would be moving away. Accordingly, early on the morning of December 18, Admiral Halsey ordered the fleet to turn south to escape the storm even more quickly.

That decision made disaster inevitable; it put the task force on a heading directly toward the center of a compact but extremely dangerous typhoon—later named Cobra—that had been following the warships from the southeast. The fleet's northwest heading had been almost exactly the same as that of the typhoon and the ships had been moving slightly faster than the eye of the storm; hence the impression of improving weather. But at midmorning on the 18th the flagship *New Jersey* encountered two dreaded signs in quick succession; the barometer began a rapid fall and the winds shifted to the north, then to the west of north. Commander Kosco knew that such a counterclockwise change could mean only one thing—a typhoon was upon them. Not only had he estimated the storm's position wrongly, but his confidence that the cold front would cause the storm to curve to the northeast proved misplaced. Typhoon Cobra simply swept the weakening front before it and bore down on the fleet. Years later, with the benefit of much more data, meteorologists would learn that a cyclone overtaking a weak cold front often intensified. But that knowledge would come far too late for Halsey's command.

By 11:30 a.m., within an hour and a half of the first unambiguous signs of a typhoon, much of Task Force 38 was laboring hard in winds of more than 115

The ABCs of Naming Storms

Agnes, Camille, Diane, Hazel, Tracy, Vera —these, and others like them, are the familiar names of tropical meteorology, employed throughout much of the world to label hurricanes, typhoons and tropical cyclones. The names are useful both for scientists and in alerting and involving the general public. Yet the practice of regularly assigning such personalized names to the great storms is a relatively recent one.

In the 19th Century only the most vicious storms were named—and then usually after the fact. Sometimes a storm was known for the island or town it ravaged, sometimes for the ship it sank. Often a storm was remembered for an event or a person associated with it.

In 1825 a hurricane that struck Puerto Rico during a religious holiday was christened Santa Ana after the saint honored on that day. A fearsome 1869 storm in Canada went into history as Saxby's Gale in honor of a British naval officer who nearly a year earlier had predicted the occurrence of a great storm. In a letter to a London newspaper he had said that the alignment of the earth, the moon and the sun would cause unusual violence.

During the early-20th Century, when weathermen first began to track tropical cyclones and predict their movements, a storm was reported by the latitude and longitude where it was spotted. But this system of numerals was too cumbersome, particularly in radio communications with ships and later with weather aircraft. In 1951 American meteorologists began to label storms with short, distinctive code words from the phonetic alphabet—Able, Baker, Charlie, etc. Although an improvement, this produced confusion when an international alphabet was introduced and radio operators used both codes to identify the same storm system.

The present system got its start in 1953, when weathermen responsible for the Caribbean adopted a system already in use in the Pacific and started giving hurricanes short, easily remembered women's names. This practice continued until 1979, when feminists persuaded the World Meteorological Organization to name storms after men as well. That same year the lists began to accommodate non-English-speaking residents of the Caribbean area; thus the first three storms of that year were named Ana, Bob and Claudette.

By 1979 the world organization was also drafting alphabetical lists of storm names for the world's major tropical storm zones. Only Asian meteorologists failed to participate; they preferred to number storms —Typhoon 1:82 for the first typhoon of 1982, Typhoon 2:82 for the second and so forth—on the theory that it was more businesslike.

miles per hour and seas rising to 70 feet. In its various maneuvers, the fleet had become spread out over an area of some 2,500 square miles, and not all of the ships encountered the full force of the typhoon. But several dozen were trapped in the heart of the storm, and for four unrelieved hours the proud vessels of the world's mightiest navy endured a nightmare of punishment. Just before noon, Admiral Halsey released his command from formation and allowed the captains to ride out the storm as best they could. By that time visibility was frequently reduced to a few feet in driving rain, and all but the largest aircraft carriers and battleships were in trouble.

Aboard the small escort carriers—tubby and top-heavy, converted from 10,000-ton freighters—the scene was one of utter chaos. The ships were bucking so wildly that planes were tearing loose from their restraining gear and crashing about the flight decks, smashing into one another and occasionally catching fire. In order to save the ships, the crews labored heroically to push the loose planes overboard. In all, nearly 150 planes were destroyed.

The worst agonies were suffered by the fleet's destroyers, the slim little "tin cans" prized more for their speed and utility than for their sea-keeping qualities. Destroyers rolled horrendously in any heavy storm, and now, despite their 40,000-horsepower engines, they were virtually unmaneuverable. The skipper of the destroyer *Hull*, Lieutenant Commander James A. Marks, recalled later how his ship, broadside to the wind, heeled over into the pounding seas. Struggling to get the ship's bow either into the wind or downwind, "I tried every possible combination of rudder and engines," said Marks. Nothing worked. The *Hull* wallowed horribly. The wind pressed the ship down until she was rolling 70 degrees; she would only barely recover before being pushed down again. It was, recalled Marks, "what I estimated to be the worst punishment any storm could offer." But the worst was still to come.

"The wind velocity increased to an unbelievable high point which I estimated to be 130 miles per hour," said Marks. "The force laid the ship steadily over on her starboard side and held her down in the water until the seas came flowing into the pilothouse itself. The ship remained on her starboard side at an angle of 80 degrees or more as the water flooded into her upper structures." The sea poured down the ship's stacks and all that Captain Marks could do was step off the bridge into the water "as the ship rolled over on her way down. Shortly after I felt the concussion of the boilers exploding under water. I concentrated my efforts thereafter on trying to keep alive." Of the 264 men on board, only 62 survived.

The *Hull* was only one of three destroyers to go down. At the height of the storm, the destroyer *Spence* took a hard roll to port, and cascading sea water short-circuited her electrical system. Without power, her rudder jammed. The crew

This map shows the breeding grounds of tropical cyclones, which can develop when the sea-surface temperature exceeds 76° F. *(shaded areas)*. The storms follow elliptical paths *(arrows)*, first moving westward with the trade winds, then either dying over land or turning eastward until they lose power over the cooler oceans of the middle latitudes. Cyclones are not spawned over the South Atlantic or the southeast Pacific, largely because their waters are too chilly, nor in the still air—the doldrums—within 5° of the Equator.

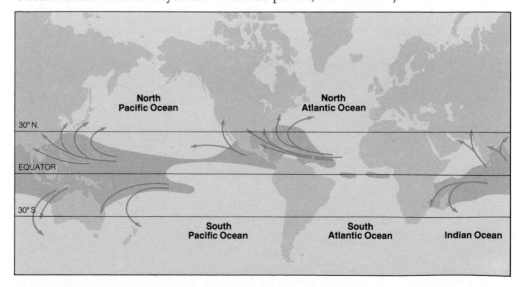

tried desperately to steer by the auxiliary system, but it was useless in the storm. The *Spence* righted, but on the next roll, with the helmsman helpless, the destroyer wallowed over even farther. More water flooded into her, and the *Spence* rolled the rest of the way over and went to the bottom. All but 24 of her 332-man crew went down with her.

A crewman on board the *Monaghan,* Joseph C. McCrane, remembered the horror belowdecks as his destroyer heeled over and lay heavily on her starboard side, gradually settling as the sea rushed in. McCrane and about 40 other men on the high port side tried to open a door, now overhead, to escape certain death. After a desperate struggle, they forced it open against the wind and, one by one, wriggled out.

As the men emerged into the screaming wind on the sea-lashed, crazily tilted deck, they scarcely had time to inflate their life vests before being washed into the boiling seas. Some, McCrane recalled, were "pounded into a pulp against the side of the ship." Others, including McCrane, were swept away; "I felt as though I were in a whirlpool. Men were knocking up against me and as I started to the surface I could feel men grabbing at me." A cresting wave caught him and swept him back onto the ship. He was trying to climb away from the waves when a comber "wrapped me around the antenna. It must have spun me around four times before it threw me loose and out into the sea again." Joseph McCrane, with nothing but a life vest, was a speck in the maelstrom of the Philippine Sea.

"Water and oil were blowing against my face," he remembered. "I was choking and beating the water like a puppy trying to stay on the surface." Someone had been able to inflate a life raft and McCrane scrambled aboard with a few others. Pitching and tossing, as much under water as on it, the little group clung to their raft as the typhoon gradually subsided. Three men died of exposure or injuries sustained while escaping from the ship, and circling sharks fed on their bodies. Three days later, on December 21, search planes spotted the tossing raft and called in a destroyer, itself badly battered, to pick up the remaining six men—the only survivors of the *Monaghan's* crew of more than 300.

All told, 82 men were picked out of the heaving seas. But 790 men were gone. Three destroyers had been sacrificed to Typhoon Cobra, and so many other ships had been damaged that the fleet could not participate in the attack on Luzon. A court of inquiry blamed the disaster on Admiral Halsey—whatever problems the weather experts had encountered, he was the responsible commander.

In an ironic reprise, about six months later Halsey was preparing to support the American forces converging on Okinawa when another typhoon, named Vi-

A U.S. destroyer wallows in a steep wave trough during a typhoon that devastated Admiral William F. Halsey's Task Force 38 in the Philippine Sea in December 1944. The captain of a destroyer escort that weathered the blow described seas "like vertical mountains," and said that at the storm's height "the tip of the adjacent ship's mast would disappear completely behind the crest of a wave."

per, approached the area. Again following his weather experts' advice, Halsey took his fleet on a course intended to escape the storm—and ran right into it. Six men were lost, 33 ships were damaged and 76 planes were destroyed.

In the aftermath of the 1944 debacle, the U.S. Navy moved swiftly to increase the number of weather stations in the western Pacific, and the Commander in Chief of the Pacific Fleet demanded that regular airborne reconnaissance of typhoons begin immediately. It was obviously a vital requirement. As it happened, plans for just such missions had been in the making for several months.

In the Gulf of Mexico the previous year, an Army Air Forces instructor, Colonel Joseph B. Duckworth, had offhandedly accomplished what no one believed possible—he had flown into the heart of a hurricane and had flown out again. Duckworth had been a veteran airline captain in peacetime. Like most pilots of his era he had earned his wings in aircraft so lacking in navigational instruments and durability that the only sensible reaction to any sight of a storm was to land immediately. But Duckworth had grasped more completely than most the import of the recent improvements in instruments and aircraft and the exigencies of a war that could not be delayed on account of weather.

Duckworth had for some time been maintaining that with proper training a modern pilot could fly in virtually any kind of weather. It was far from an idle contention; by 1943 he had been training Army pilots for more than two years and in February had taken command of the first Air Force instrument training school.

On the morning of July 27, Duckworth heard a weather bureau report that a hurricane was in the Gulf of Mexico, approaching Galveston, Texas. It was an opportunity to make his case for instrument flying, and along with navigator Lieutenant Ralph O'Hair, Duckworth promptly took off in a single-engined AT-6 trainer and headed for the storm.

The little plane was first assaulted by fringe winds that made the craft buck, then by torrents of rain. Black clouds turned day into night. The plane droned on into the outskirts of the hurricane-force winds, plunging and soaring in the updrafts and downdrafts. Duckworth, flying blind and relying solely on his instruments, fought to keep the little trainer aloft as it rammed into the full force of the hurricane winds. The AT-6 now bounced about virtually out of control, sideslipping and leaping and diving hundreds of feet as the gusts struck it broadside. Then the plane suddenly leveled out in an utterly calm sky. Duckworth and O'Hair were in the eye of the storm.

The tragic course changes and flawed meteorology that led Halsey's fleet into the center of Typhoon Cobra can be seen on this map of the Philippine Sea representing three days in mid-December, 1944. The weather officer's estimate *(black line)* put the typhoon far to the east and curving northwestward. But the typhoon's track *(green line)* actually was to the south; Halsey's generally southward headings *(orange line),* intended to escape the storm, took the task force directly toward it.

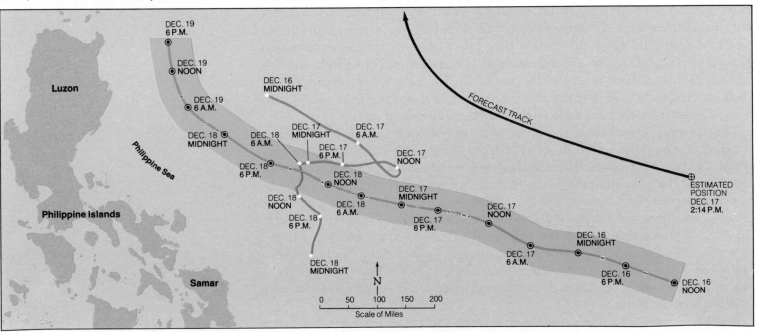

Above them was a clear blue sky. Below, they could see the Texas countryside. Then, just as suddenly, the blackness closed in again, the winds seized the plane and the rain pummeled it. Duckworth and O'Hair went on another wild roller-coaster ride through the other side of the cyclonic storm. But the little training plane roared through the hurricane and out into clear weather again. O'Hair got his bearings, and Duckworth flew back to Bryan Field.

There, Lieutenant William Jones-Burdick, the base weather officer, expressed his disappointment at being left behind on the historic flight. Duckworth told him to hop in, took off and flew toward the hurricane again, Jones-Burdick making what measurements he could while bouncing about in his safety harness. He managed to record a few observations of temperature, air turbulence, cloud thickness and barometric pressure as Duckworth flew through the eye and back to the base.

On both flights the airmen found that as they penetrated the outer rim of the storm they encountered heavy rain and severe turbulence, the rain causing severe static interference with their radio communications. Then as they moved deeper into the storm system the precipitation and turbulence moderated, only to increase substantially again just before they broke into the eye. It was the first glimpse of the workings of a hurricane above the surface, and it brought the first hint of the monumental complexities ahead. This storm was not a homogeneous circle of wind and cloud as many had supposed, but a seething caldron of conditions ranging from the near calm to the unbelievably chaotic.

The observations whetted the thirst of meteorologists for more knowledge about what was going on in the heart of hurricanes, particularly at various altitudes. The scientists believed that if they could study the winds aloft in a hurricane they could make better forecasts of its behavior; it was the kind of information only aircraft could obtain, and Duckworth had shown that it could be done. Observations from several more flights into 1943 hurricanes were forwarded to the U.S. Weather Bureau. By the beginning of 1944, Army and Navy flight crews had been assigned to hurricane-hunting duty in the Atlantic and Caribbean under the auspices of a joint weather bureau-armed forces hurricane center in Miami. And with the impetus of the Halsey disaster, similar assignments were soon made in the Pacific.

By October of 1945 Army and Navy airmen and meteorologists had flown hundreds of missions into Pacific typhoons and Atlantic hurricanes. And while they found no immediate answers to the problems of forecasting storm tracks, they collected enough information for the theorists to puzzle over for years.

In many parts of the storm system, the airborne hurricane hunters found fewer sharp gusts and less turbulence than they had expected—in fact, experienced pilots found conditions to be less severe than they had encountered on the periphery of thunderstorms. They found that the air in the eye was quiet and smooth at most altitudes, and that it was much warmer than that of the clouds surrounding it. This new data posed a challenge to the scientists—to adapt their theories of hurricane formation and behavior to account for the information—and raised new questions before the old ones could be resolved.

While the burgeoning information challenged the theorists and defied the forecasters, it had immediate practical value for the fliers—it helped them chart the best route into and out of the cloud masses, and thus perfect their tracking technique. At first the pilots' procedure was to get as high as their aircraft would fly before penetrating the eye, then descend in its relative calm to take pressure, temperature and humidity readings at various altitudes.

Soon the Navy and the Air Force developed different techniques to suit their different missions; the Navy wanted to know about sea conditions and wind strength at the surface, while the Air Force was naturally interested in conditions aloft. Navy pilots flew their twin-engined PB4Y-2 Privateers into the hurricanes at altitudes of between 300 and 700 feet. They found that below 300 feet, turbulence increased to the danger point. If they flew above 700 feet they spent most of their time in the clouds, which was almost as bad. Not only did the clouds prevent them from observing the condition of the sea, but since lowering pressure toward the center of the storm caused altimeters to indicate progressively higher altitudes, a pilot maintaining level flight by his instruments could fly right into the sea. Radar altimeters would later alleviate the danger, but in the meanwhile it was urgently necessary for the low-flying Navy pilots to keep the surface in view. Navy pilots approached the system from the left rear quadrant, crossed the eye, and flew out of the storm.

Air Force B-25 flights entered and left the hurricane's eye at about 8,000 feet and seldom flew below 2,000 feet. Because of their interest in recording conditions at higher altitudes, and their ongoing research into the nature of the hurricane's eye, Air Force pilots developed a different flight pattern from that of the Navy. They flew directly through the eye of a hurricane from the same quadrant, turned left to get ahead of it, then turned again to recross the eye, flying out of

Her nose broken by huge waves, the carrier *Hornet* returns to San Francisco for repairs after Task Force 38's second punishing encounter with a typhoon in less than six months. Meteorologists judged the second storm, Viper, to be smaller than Cobra in area but more intense, with 140-mph winds.

the hurricane through the section they had entered. All pilots learned to avoid, insofar as they could, the areas within the hurricane system that contained the worst of the turbulence and precipitation.

The greatest enemy of the hurricane hunters, after the physical danger to their aircraft posed by the turbulence, was the severe precipitation static within the eye. Aloft in the maelstrom, the only way the fliers could determine their position was to take bearings on distant radio navigation stations. When static made that impossible, the crew was blind; they could neither report the exact location of the eye nor communicate their various atmospheric readings. After two hours of static-induced radio blackout in a Caribbean hurricane, a member of one flight crew greeted the first sight of the surface as they roared out of the clouds with the wry comment: "We are still lost, but we are making excellent time."

Despite the difficulties, the hurricane hunters were able by the mid-1940s to pinpoint, day by day, where a hurricane was located and what it was doing. With that kind of information available, there would never again be an excuse for a debacle like the 1938 killer hurricane that roared into New England completely without warning.

The difficulty and the utility of the hurricane hunters' job were amply demonstrated in September of 1945 during one of the most violent Atlantic hurricanes in history. The hurricane was born over western Africa during the first few days of September, gathered strength near the Cape Verde Islands and headed westward. Flying in specially instrumented B-25 twin-engined bombers, hurricane hunters spotted the huge storm on September 12 several hundred miles east of Antigua and kept a close watch as it headed toward Florida.

The first airborne penetration of the hurricane encountered winds exceeding 120 miles per hour. Despite all precautions, the flight crew was subjected to

Air Force hurricane hunters based in Bermuda line up in front of their specially equipped B-29 before a weather reconnaissance flight in 1952. The squadron emblem, a wry comment on the pioneering nature of the missions, is a tiny airman riding a magic carpet and relying on a crystal ball to guide him through the storm.

buffeting such as the men had never before experienced—and the storm was not yet at full strength. By the 15th, conditions inside the hurricane were truly awesome. Lieutenant James P. Dalton was the navigator on a B-25 that took off from West Palm Beach, Florida, as the leading edge of the storm came ashore. He was a veteran of 1,500 hours of hurricane reconnaissance, but he remembered this one as "absolutely the worst.

"One minute this plane, seemingly under control, would suddenly wrench itself free, throw itself into a vertical bank and head straight for the steaming white sea below. An instant later it was on the other wing, this time climbing with its nose down at an ungodly speed. I stood on my hands as much as I did on my feet. Rain was so heavy it was as if we were flying through the sea like a submarine. Navigation was practically impossible. For not a minute could we say we were moving in any single direction—at one time I recorded 28 degrees drift, two minutes later it was from the opposite direction almost as strong. At one time our pressure altimeter was indicating 2,600 feet due to the drop in pressure, when we actually were at 700 feet. At this time the bottom fell out. I don't know how close we came to the sea but it was far too close to suit my fancy."

Airsick for the first time in his career, desperately frightened, Dalton prayed for deliverance from the storm: "I vouched if I could come out alive I would never fly again." But by the time he was back on the ground after the five-hour flight Dalton had recovered his perspective.

The hurricane crossed the southern Florida peninsula on September 16 and moved northward into Georgia on the 17th. Lieutenant George Gray, a weather officer on a flight that observed the hurricane battering the Georgia coast, described his aircraft's encounter with the rain: "It looked absolutely black, as if a sudden darkness had set in in that part of the sky. The blackness seemed to hang straight down like a thick dark curtain from a solid cloud deck at about 15,000 feet. I kept thinking, 'We're not actually going into that.' We did though.

"The nose usually leaks and a soaking on a trip is not at all unusual, but this was different. Where the plexiglass meets the floor section there was a regular fountain about six inches high that flooded the whole area. The noise was terrific. It pounded and crushed against the top and sides until we thought it would all collapse in on us." Fortunately, the worst assaults of water and turbulence were experienced just outside the eye; as they circled in the welcome quiet of the eye itself there was time for the crew to radio back their vital reports, enjoy a quick cup of coffee and brace themselves for the flight out.

Escorted by the weather reconnaissance aircraft and preceded by their warnings, the great hurricane intensified briefly just off the coast of Georgia but then quickly moderated to a heavy rainstorm that lumbered northward through the mid-Atlantic states, New England and New Brunswick before moving out into the North Atlantic on September 20.

The fliers could measure the worth of the risks they took in terms of lives saved. One rough estimate was provided by a comparison of fatalities with property damage. In 1925 a hurricane that did $10 million worth of damage could be expected, on the average, to claim 160 lives. After 1946, thanks in large measure to the warnings provided by the hurricane hunters, the average number of deaths in a similarly destructive hurricane was reduced to four.

The flights also continued to provide unprecedented information about the nature of the hurricane and its terrors. Beginning in 1945, weather radar was installed on board storm-hunting aircraft and soon revealed the actual, as opposed to theoretical or deduced, shape of the storm. In fact, radar aboard Task Force 38 had shown a clear profile of Halsey's typhoon in 1944, but no one understood what it meant. Such sightings were rare on board surface vessels, but the signals from the hurricane hunters' airborne radar were reflected by the precipitation surrounding the eye and revealed it clearly on the radar screen. Thus

The placid-looking cloudscape above a Caribbean hurricane belies the violence within as a B-29 weather plane, flying at 30,000 feet, approaches the storm on October 7, 1946, to conduct high-altitude research. The crewman silhouetted at left was assigned to watch for oil leaks as the aircraft flew through turbulence.

Perched in the nose of a modified B-29 bomber, two U.S. Air Force meteorologists fly through a Caribbean hurricane in 1946. The observer on the right bends over a drift meter, which, by measuring the aircraft's deviation from its set course, enables him to estimate wind speed and direction. The man on the left monitors the aircraft's altitude on a radio altimeter, thus gauging the storm's violent updrafts and downdrafts.

the flight crews did not have to feel their way through the turbulent inward spiral of the winds but could fly directly toward the storm's center.

As an unexpected bonus the radar revealed something that no one had ever suspected from previous observations—that the areas of heavy precipitation and turbulence in the storm system were tightly organized strips that spiraled inward toward the eye of the hurricane. These octopus-like arms within the storm were hundreds of miles long, but often only a few miles wide, and pilots soon learned how to stay out of the rainbands, as they came to be known, as long as possible.

The flights became ever more frequent, and before the theorists could work out an explanation for one set of observations, the aircraft would be back with another. In 1947 a crew in a B-29 Superfortress set out from Bermuda to probe the upper limits of a hurricane and to try to find out what was steering it. The meteorologists believed that the clouds sloped upward away from the eye, to a maximum height of about 35,000 feet. But the high-flying B-29 was almost to 40,000 feet before it topped the cloud bank—and the clouds rose even higher in the direction of the storm's center. The eye, it turned out, was not a broad, inverted cone but a tightly organized cylinder all the way to the top.

Weather bureau meteorologist Robert H. Simpson, who never lost an opportunity to ride with the hurricane hunters, described another unexpected phenomenon encountered by the high-flying B-29s. "Through this fog of cirrostratus clouds in which we were travelling at 250 miles an hour there loomed from time to time ghost-like structures rising like huge white marble monuments. Each time we passed through one of these shafts the leading edge of the wing accumulated an amazing extra coating of rime ice. We were so close to the center of the storm by the time the icing was discovered that the shafts were too numerous to avoid." As the ice accumulated on the wings, it slowed the aircraft to within three miles per hour of its stalling speed and an inevitable plunge into the hurricane-racked sea. Gingerly, the pilot put the aircraft's nose down and managed a long, flat, harrowing glide to safety.

Simpson would later explain that the shafts were rising fountains of supercooled water—liquid water chilled far below its freezing point without solidifying. Contact with the aircraft wing changed this supercooled water instantly to ice. The presence of supercooled water at the extremely low temperatures in the shafts defied the known laws of physics. And the forces necessary to set up the

A bird's-eye view shows the different flight paths followed by Air Force *(solid line)* and Navy *(dotted line)* hurricane hunters on research missions in the 1950s. Both entered the storm from the left rear quadrant, where the wind and rain are least violent. The Air Force technique was to fly a clover-leaf pattern at 8,000 feet and again at 14,000 feet to cover as much of the storm as possible. The Navy, being primarily interested in sea conditions, flew at 300-to-700-foot altitudes to circle the eye, then usually exited near the point of entry.

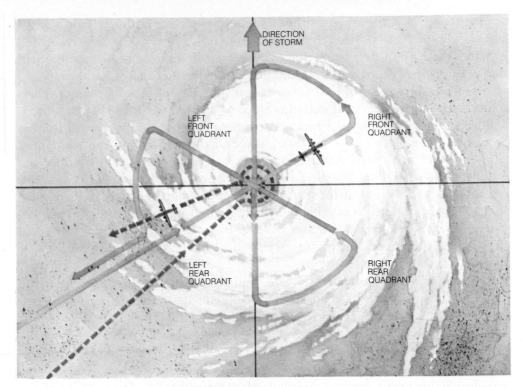

circulation that could create such wonders were beyond comprehension. Simpson could only exclaim in wonder, "this was fantastic. Unbelievable."

The volumes of new information allowed researchers to construct a much clearer picture of the hurricane's typical patterns of wind speeds, changing barometric pressures, distribution of rainfall and varieties of cloud formations. But the patterns were still too vast, the data too sketchy and too often contradictory to permit final answers to the basic questions of why a hurricane formed, what steered it, and exactly how the massive quantities of air were circulated in and through it. Rather, the new details raised new questions, and created an even greater need for still more data. In fact, as a professor of meteorology at the University of Chicago, Herbert Riehl, would say: "Our knowledge regarding the wind distribution within tropical storms and the dynamical laws that guide the air from the outskirts to the center of the cyclone is so deficient as to be deplorable."

The German-born Riehl, not the sort of man to content himself with deploring things, soon had his chance to correct the deficiencies. In 1944 he was dispatched by the University of Chicago's famed Carl-Gustaf Rossby to the school's new institute of tropical meteorology at the University of Puerto Rico. It was a perfect location for the study of Atlantic and Caribbean hurricanes, and Riehl swiftly moved into the forefront of tropical-cyclone research—where he would remain for a generation.

For some years, a handful of meteorologists had been attempting to apply to tropical cyclones the theories of Norway's renowned Bergen school of meteorologists. The experts of the Bergen school had found that the cyclonic storms they studied were born in fronts—narrow bands of dramatic discontinuity between air masses. But this theory, which had proved so valuable in understanding storms of the middle latitudes, simply did not apply to hurricanes: The airborne hurricane hunters had found that fronts clearly did not form in the tropics. If fronts were not responsible for the development of hurricanes, what then was the mechanism involved?

Riehl soon confirmed and expanded on the discovery of a colleague, Gordon E. Dunn, who combined an extraordinary ability as a forecaster with a keen interest in research. While analyzing data collected in the Caribbean Islands Dunn had frequently noticed a progression, from east to west across the area, of a relatively rapid sequence of rising, then falling, barometric pressure readings. It was as if a series of low-pressure waves were rolling through the area.

Armed with fresh data from the upper air and from vessels far at sea, Riehl soon realized that Dunn had identified a unique phenomenon that appeared to have a role in the genesis of hurricanes. These undulations of reduced atmospheric pressure, and the banks of cumulus cloud and thunderstorms they produced, could be found marching in a more or less regular procession westward from as far east as Africa, across the Atlantic, through the Caribbean, and sometimes across the neck of Central America and out into the Pacific. Each summer and autumn there were about 100 of these easterly waves, as they came to be called, and about seven or eight of them turned into full-fledged hurricanes. Like most discoveries about hurricanes, this knowledge raised more questions than it answered. Why did so few hurricanes develop from so many easterly waves? And why did the number of hurricanes vary so much more widely from year to year than the number of waves?

As Riehl searched for answers in the conditions that prevailed in the earliest stages of hurricanes, he was able to define more of the things that had to come together in this already complex mix of conditions. Two of the most important were the arrival of an easterly wave and the presence of an external forcing mechanism. The easterly wave of low pressure, when it encountered vigorous convection over a warm ocean, energized the forces already at work and turned the cumulus clouds into towering cumulonimbus thunderheads. If, when the thunderheads had built up to 40,000 feet or higher, they encountered strong winds that whisked the warm air away—Riehl's forcing mechanism—the circulation was accelerated even more, and the birth of a hurricane was possible.

But while Riehl could explain these elements that contributed to the genesis of a hurricane, he could not say precisely how or why they came together. The frustrating reality remained that all the elements of his theory often came together without resulting in the ominous preliminary swirl of a hurricane—and a hurricane sometimes formed without the presence of every element. Later research would show that nothing like the easterly wave was present at the birth of hurricanes in other parts of the world.

Riehl devoted his life to enlarging and refining his theories to accommodate the ever-growing body of data recorded in hurricane after hurricane. Still, none of the considerable advances he made could foretell the unprecedented onslaught of vicious hurricanes that would strike the eastern United States in the 1950s.

The first of the period's monster storms was discovered in August of 1954. In 1953 the U.S. Weather Bureau had begun assigning female names to tropical storms to simplify communications (pages 92-93). This one, the third of the season, was named Carol. It formed over the Bahamas and moved almost straight north to batter New England on a course strikingly similar to that of the 1938 hurricane; the major difference was that Carol's eye made its landfall at the eastern tip of Long Island, and the worst of the winds, those in the northeastern quadrant, remained at sea. Though property damage approached half a billion dollars, the highest ever in a hurricane up to that time, the loss of life, thanks to timely warnings, was held to only 60 deaths.

Less than a fortnight later, during the second week of September, Hurricane Edna roared out of the Atlantic to deluge New York City with five inches of rain in 14 hours. Edna's center moved northward along the coasts of Massachusetts and Maine, then into Nova Scotia, leaving behind 22 people dead and property damage totaling $50 million. It was already an extraordinary year in the history of Atlantic hurricanes, but all that had happened so far was merely a prelude.

On October 5, 1954, Hurricane Hazel, one of the mightiest tropical storms ever to strike North America, was born near Grenada in the Lesser Antilles. After building up and moving northwestward through the Caribbean Sea for a week, Hazel struck Haiti on October 12, destroying three towns and killing perhaps

A Fantastic Pinwheel of Pacific Cyclones

In this satellite photograph taken in August 1974, twin Pacific hurricanes Kirsten (*top right*) and Ione (*bottom left*) are linked by cloud as they pinwheel about each other in a counterclockwise direction.

When two tropical cyclones approach within 900 miles of each other, they are frequently attracted into orbits around a common center, much like planets in the solar system. This curious interaction of cyclones—which occurs about once a year in the Pacific and far less frequently in the Atlantic—is called the Fujiwara effect after a pioneer of Japanese meteorology, Sakuhei Fujiwara, who in 1921 was the first to study the phenomenon.

Though Fujiwara was unable to explain all of the forces that draw the great storms together, he did analyze a wide range of effects. He found, for example, that if the cyclones were of approximately equal size, they would revolve around a center midway between the two. However, if they were unequal in size, the center would be nearer the larger storm. When this happened, the smaller cyclone would increase speed dramatically until it revolved in the same orbit as the larger one.

1,000 people. The storm was so huge that it spread across an area of 9,000 square miles; at the same time that it was battering Haiti, it was dumping 12 inches of rain on Puerto Rico, 500 miles to the east. Hazel then curved north, drenched the Bahamas, and intensified until its winds reached 126 miles per hour.

On the morning of October 15, Hazel hit the U.S. mainland near Myrtle Beach, South Carolina. The storm tide reached 17 feet above mean low water in some places, and destroyed every fishing pier along a 170-mile stretch of beach. Coastal cities and towns were devastated. The storm destroyed homes, hotels and office buildings worth $60 million on the coast of the Carolinas alone; out of 275 buildings in the business district of Garden City, South Carolina, only three remained unscathed. Because of the improved warnings, however, only 19 people lost their lives.

Surprisingly, considering that it was over land, Hazel then intensified; it went on a rampage through North Carolina, Virginia, Maryland, Pennsylvania and central New York State. It brought torrential rains and record winds to Washington, D.C., and New York City during the latter stages of the rush hours. The control towers at both LaGuardia and Newark Airports were abandoned for a time as they swayed in gusts of more than 100 miles per hour. But both cities had taken precautions; in Washington government workers had been allowed to go home early, and in New York hurricane warnings had been broadcast and emergency services were on alert. Overall, in the United States, the storm claimed only 95 lives—though property damage reached a quarter of a billion dollars.

Hazel then smashed into Canada. In Toronto, after seven inches of rain fell in one day, the rampaging waters of the Humber and Credit Rivers killed 80 people and left 4,000 families homeless. Property damage in Canada totaled $100 million by the time the remnants of Hazel moved out over the Atlantic on October 18. Days later, the storm was still producing strong winds and heavy rains somewhere north of Scandinavia.

There was no respite for New England the next year. The two hurricanes that came ashore in 1955 were not particularly violent in their wind and storm-surge effects, but they brought prodigious quantities of rain to the area. The first, Hurricane Connie, struck in mid-August, saturating the ground and filling the rivers. The second, Diane, arrived a few days later and brought deadly floods at the peak of the tourist season. One creek near Stroudsberg, Pennsylvania, rose so high so fast that 50 people were drowned. In all, more than 190 people died, and the property damages were the highest for any natural disaster in American history up to that time—more than $1.6 billion.

The year 1956 passed without incident, but on June 27, 1957, a small, intense hurricane named Audrey came ashore from the Gulf of Mexico near the Louisiana-Texas border. Forecasters had been watching it closely for two days and had warned residents of low-lying areas to evacuate. But the meteorologists failed to predict a sudden acceleration of the storm that occurred during the last 12 hours before landfall. (It was also claimed later that they had not issued strong enough warnings.) Large numbers of people were unprepared when the hurricane hit, and nearly 400 perished in the 100-mile-per-hour winds and 12-foot storm surge that ravaged coastal Louisiana.

The 1950s also produced some extraordinary tropical cyclones in the Pacific. In 1953 a typhoon destroyed one third of the Japanese industrial city of Nagoya on the main island of Honshu, leaving one million people without homes and 100 dead. The next year, 1,600 people died in a monstrous storm that struck the northern Japanese island of Hokkaido. Five years later, in September of 1959, Typhoon Vera, the worst in modern Japanese history, killed almost 4,500 people, destroyed 40,000 homes and left 1.5 million people homeless on Honshu. A month later, a fierce hurricane slammed into the Pacific coast of Mexico—a rare event—and killed 2,000 people.

There were few clues to what might have caused this unprecedented decade of carnage by tropical cyclones. Students of long-term storm patterns could chart—but could not account for—some fascinating trends, particularly in the western Atlantic, where a rapidly expanding coastal population and sea trade had provided better early hurricane records than in other areas.

For 100 years, an average of five hurricanes had formed in the Atlantic each season; however, individual years varied dramatically. During 1925, for instance, only one hurricane had occurred, while in 1926 there were eight. Nevertheless, there was an apparent 40-year trend during the century; from 1895 to 1931 the numbers tended to be below normal, with a low point in the years 1927 to 1931. After 1931, which saw but two hurricanes, there was a sharp increase to six in 1932 and nine in 1933. And the average tended to remain above normal for the next 40 years.

Statistics on the hurricanes spawned in the other tropical breeding grounds were much less complete than those for the North Atlantic, and would remain so until the advent of the all-seeing weather satellites in the 1960s. It was known that the western North Pacific could expect about 20 typhoons a year, with an occasional supertyphoon sprawling across an area equal to that of the continental United States. Meteorologists speculated that these immense storm systems were the result of the longer reach of ocean, unobstructed by large land masses, that existed in the Pacific.

The North Indian Ocean could expect some six tropical cyclones a year in two annual seasons—late spring and early autumn. Little was known about the frequency of tropical cyclones in the waters around Australia or in the South Pacific and South Indian Oceans except that they were frequent and powerful. What was known about the South Atlantic—that not a single hurricane had ever been reported there—was, and remains, another mystery. It may be too small an ocean, or too cold, or the wind patterns may be wrong for hurricane formation.

The hurricane disasters in the North Atlantic in the early 1950s had one beneficial effect. In the summer of 1956, the U.S. government commenced an all-out effort to unravel the secrets of the great storms. The National Hurricane Research Project, as it was called, was designed and led by the weather bureau's Robert Simpson, the veteran hurricane hunter who had flown into dozens of tropical cyclones in the late 1940s and early 1950s.

Simpson brought together the best people and the most advanced technology available to the weather bureau, the armed services, and half a dozen major universities and leading research organizations. Two B-50 piston-engined bombers and one B-47 jet bomber were packed with navigation and meteorological instruments until they fairly bristled with antennas and sampling devices. The aircraft were capable of measuring winds, temperatures, pressures, humidity and the liquid content of clouds; they could record both photographic and radar images of the hurricane's innards; and under Simpson's direction there was often more than one aircraft probing a hurricane at the same time, measuring conditions at different altitudes.

The infusion of new leadership, equipment and money doubled and redoubled the flow of incoming measurements. It made the flood of information produced by the original hurricane hunters seem like a trickle in retrospect. There was too much data to be handled by individuals; much of it was recorded automatically on board the aircraft on punched cards for transcribing and processing by the newly available digital computers. The effort was so massive and the techniques so advanced that most meteorologists believed success in cracking the innermost secrets of the hurricane was at hand. It was not.

There were, to be sure, some new insights into the mechanisms of hurricanes. The aerial measurements revealed that the water content of the hurricane's clouds was surprisingly high—more than twice what it had been supposed to be; this water represented an enormous energy reserve for the hurricane that some meteo-

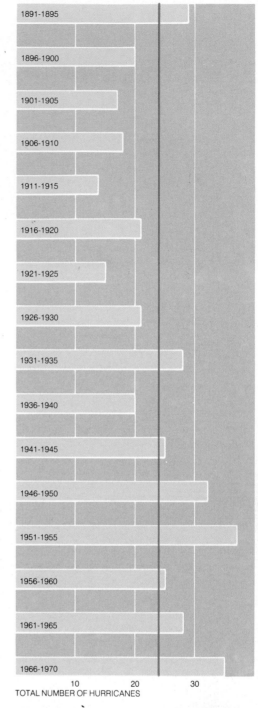

TOTAL NUMBER OF HURRICANES

This chart reflects the varying frequency of Atlantic hurricanes over an 80-year period. Each horizontal bar indicates the total number of hurricanes that occurred in a five-year period; the solid vertical line represents the average number of hurricanes—23—for an average five-year period. A pattern is suggested by the dip in totals to below average between 1900 and 1930, and the increase to above average between 1935 and 1970. If repeated in the future, such a pattern might indicate a 30-to-40-year cycle in hurricane frequency.

No one knows exactly where or when the practice originated. Perhaps it began in Bermuda or Florida, where residents had lived through so many hurricanes that the more daredevil among them became contemptuous of the great storms. In any case, by the 1950s, it was fashionable for thrill seekers to hold "hurricane parties." Instead of evacuating, these people elected to stock up with food and drink and invite their friends over to ride out the whirlwind.

So it was in the beach-front Richelieu Apartments in Pass Christian, Mississippi, on August 17, 1969. The weather bureau had issued urgent warnings of the approach of Hurricane Camille. The forecasters had labeled it an extremely dangerous storm, characterized by a tightly packed vortex containing 200-mile-per-hour winds.

Nevertheless, 12 people gathered on the third floor of the Richelieu to celebrate the coming of Camille. It is likely that they expected only an exhilarating blow and spectacular surf. The weather bureau had predicted that the center of the storm would strike the Florida panhandle, 100 miles to the east.

But Camille veered westward and within the day came roaring ashore at Pass Christian. The Richelieu Apartments were directly in the path of the worst winds and a storm surge that rose 19 feet above the high-tide line.

Aside from the 12 partygoers, another dozen people were in the apartment house that evening. At least two of them, Mary Ann Gerlach and her husband Fritz, were preparing to join the celebrants. "We had been in hurricanes in Florida," she said later. "You get off work and it's—you know—party time."

The Gerlachs never made it to the party. Waves hammered at the picture window in their second-floor living room. "We heard an awful popping sound as the windows went. We held our shoulders to the bedroom door to try to keep the water from coming in. But in about five minutes the bed was floating halfway to the ceiling. You could feel the building swaying like we were in a boat," said Mrs. Gerlach.

Somehow, Mrs. Gerlach managed to swim out a window. She saw her husband disappear beneath the waves. And then, looking back, she watched in horror as the entire Richelieu building collapsed like a child's sand castle into the maelstrom.

The rest of the night was etched in Mrs. Gerlach's memory. She recalled grabbing some wreckage and being driven along by winds so strong that she could scarcely breathe. At last she was deposited in a treetop almost five miles from the beach, and there she stayed until her rescue the following morning.

Of the 24 people in the apartment house, she was the sole survivor. Everyone else had either drowned or been crushed to death when the building crumbled. Mrs. Gerlach supplied their epitaphs when she said: "Whenever there's a hurricane warning now, I get out with all the rest."

Located on the beach at Pass Christian, Mississippi, the Richelieu apartment complex *(above, left)* is a sun-worshipper's paradise in this aerial photo taken from a sales brochure. But it proved a death-trap for 23 people who remained when Hurricane Camille swept ashore in August 1969, reducing the luxury building to rubble *(above)*.

rologists thought offered possibilities for modification efforts. The scientists also were surprised to find that cool, dry air was blowing right through the middle levels of the hurricane in a process they called ventilation. This mixing of cool, dry air with the warm, moist air of the storm's heat engine acted, in effect, like a brake on the hurricane's development; the more ventilation the less intense the storm would be at its worst; the less ventilation the fiercer the storm would eventually be.

In addition to yielding such fascinating, albeit baffling, bits of information, the data changed the scientists' overall perception of the energy cycles within a hurricane. The numbers showed that the latent heat released by condensation could not by itself provide enough energy to drive the storm; there had to be a significant source of heat energy at the surface. In fact, there appeared to be a strong relationship between maximum winds at the center and the temperature differential between the sea and air at the surface; in broad terms, the warmer the sea relative to the air, the more energy was imparted to the cyclone and the higher its winds.

Moreover, the computations showed that friction between the wind and the surface—even the ground—was not as significant as many had thought in slowing hurricane winds. Indeed, more energy was lost to friction between turbulent parcels of free air near the core of the storm than between the wind and the ground. And what acted to dissipate the storm was primarily the loss of contact with the warm ocean that fueled the heat engine.

The National Hurricane Research Project—which in 1959 was merged with the Hurricane Forecast Center in Miami to form the National Hurricane Center—had four objectives outlined at the outset by Simpson. It made vast and exciting advances along the lines of the first goal, which was "to investigate the distribution of energy in the hurricane and to develop an accurate energy budget for the storm." But its other objectives—to determine how hurricanes worked, how they could be modified and the specific forces that caused them to move—remained out of reach.

By now, the hurricane researchers were awash in data—and there was much more to come. In April of 1960 the first weather satellite was rocketed into orbit. The Television and Infrared Observation Satellite, or TIROS, offered unprecedented visual and heat-sensing surveillance of the tropics. It took only a few days for TIROS to confirm its value. On April 10, satellite photos pinpointed a hitherto unsuspected typhoon in the South Pacific 800 miles east of Brisbane, Australia. "What this means," said Francis W. Reichelderfer, Chief of the U.S. Weather Bureau, "is that hurricanes spawned anywhere over the vast oceanic areas can be detected much earlier than ever before possible."

It also meant that previous estimates of global hurricane activity had to be drastically revised. The satellites discovered that 80 tropical cyclones swirled

Recorded 28 years apart, these two images of hurricanes illustrate the marked advances in weather observation techniques in recent times. The 1951 radar image of Typhoon Marge (*left*) was made by bouncing pulsed radio waves from an airplane transmitter off water droplets in the hurricane; the brightest spots on the resulting picture indicated areas of heaviest precipitation. The infrared picture of Typhoon Vera (*above*), transmitted by satellite in 1979, produced a far more detailed image; color added by computer helped meteorologists to gauge both temperature and rainfall in different parts of the hurricane, and to estimate the storm's strength, maturity and course.

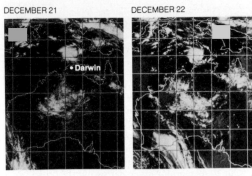

DECEMBER 21

DECEMBER 22

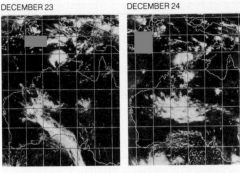

DECEMBER 23

DECEMBER 24

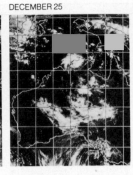

DECEMBER 25

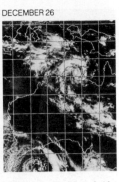

DECEMBER 26

Cyclone Tracy's leisurely southwestward course over the Arafura Sea in December 1974, seen in this series of U.S. satellite photos, suggested at first that it posed no threat to the coastal city of Darwin, Australia. Even at midmorning on December 24, when its eye had contracted and Tracy had become more intense, forecasters thought that the storm would bypass the city. But later in the day, Tracy suddenly hooked around to the southeast and by the time the next photo was taken on Christmas Day, it had flattened Darwin. By December 26, Tracy had dissipated considerably.

The shattered remains of Darwin, Australia, bake in the summer sun after Cyclone Tracy's Christmas Day onslaught in 1974. Tracy's winds, which reached 150 mph, pummeled the city for more than four hours, reducing 8,000 homes to rubble and forcing the evacuation of most of Darwin's 48,000 inhabitants.

across the world's oceans each year—twice the earlier estimates. But while TIROS and succeedingly more advanced weather satellites added greatly to meteorologists' knowledge, the satellites had inherent limitations that once again forestalled the dawn of a new era in hurricane prediction.

The scientists soon realized that a satellite picture was a portrait not of the dynamic workings of the hurricane itself, but of the dense overlying cloud that was emerging from the hurricane—its exhaust, as it were, spiraling outward from the storm. Certain broad inferences could be drawn from the behavior of the cloud cover, one of the most valuable being that a marked contraction of the visible eye of the hurricane indicated a pronounced intensification of the storm. But the satellites were looking at the hurricane's upper fringes, not into its heart. That their contribution to forecasting remained problematical was dramatically demonstrated many years after satellite observations had become commonplace.

On December 21, 1974, weather satellite pictures showed that a large mass of clouds in the Arafura Sea between Australia and New Guinea had taken on the ominous circular form of a developing typhoon. For the next three days the typhoon intensified and traveled slowly and steadily southwestward over open water toward the Indian Ocean, and forecasters assured Australians that the storm would pass 60 miles offshore. On December 24, Cyclone Tracy, as it was named, suddenly intensified and changed course to the southeast, and at 4 a.m. on the 25th slammed into Darwin, the capital of Australia's Northern Territory. The city of 48,000 people was almost completely destroyed and 50 people were killed by the 150-mile-per-hour winds.

Daily satellite observations of Tracy did not contribute to any forecast of its sudden change of course, but did permit warnings to be issued promptly after the fact. By then, however, it was Christmas Eve, and a large majority of Darwin residents later confessed that they did not take the warnings seriously enough, either because they were involved with Christmas celebrations or because they simply did not believe that the unprecedented threat was real.

In addition to greatly improving the monitoring of dangerous tropical cyclones, the satellites contributed new details about the storms' physical characteristics and tracks. But even with that information added to the continuing flow from airborne reconnaissance flights, ships and ground stations, the meteorologists still could not explain why these great and erratic storms acted as they did. One ray of hope came from the fast-growing technology of high-speed computers. It seemed logical that if any analytical tool could assess the virtually infinite variables of tropical meteorology, it would be the computer. Accordingly, much of the effort of hurricane research from the 1960s onward was devoted to computer programs capable of digesting everything known about hurricanes, isolating the patterns, and thus making it possible to forecast what would happen next.

The first attempts, incorporating all the relevant mathematical formulas quantifying heat transfers, energy exchanges, fluid dynamics and so on, were designed to predict the birth of a hurricane. They could be said to have worked too well. When the computers were fed the data recorded in any tropical disturbance, of which there are more than 100 each year in the Atlantic Ocean alone, the elec-

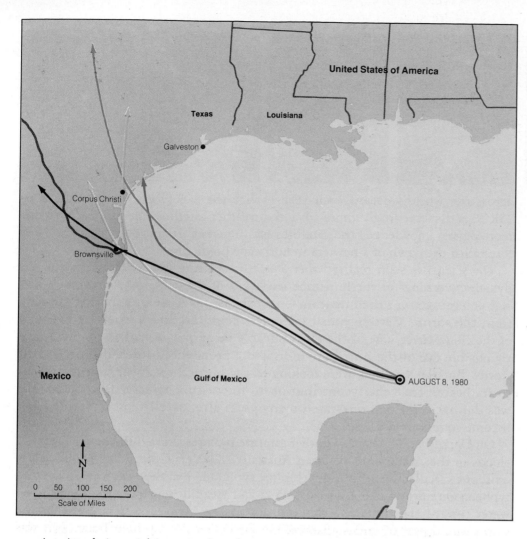

The colored lines on this map represent the August 8, 1980, efforts of four different weather service computer programs to predict the course of Hurricane Allen over a 72-hour period; the black line traces Allen's actual path. Although computers are clearly fallible as hurricane forecasters, their analyses are swift and of considerable value to meteorologists in narrowing the broad range of possible courses for each new storm.

tronic wizards invariably arrived at the conclusion that a full hurricane was in the making. The programmers returned to their calculations.

During the 1960s and 1970s, scientists developed several computer models—including mathematical simulations of hurricane processes—designed to respond to data on an existing storm by projecting its course. Some stored millions of pieces of information on the tracks of past hurricanes and the atmospheric conditions that surrounded them. As observations from an existing storm came in, these computers made lightning-fast searches for similar sets of circumstances, and made their projection. Others applied countless formulas of thermodynamics to the observed conditions in a hurricane and did what Vilhelm Bjerknes had wanted to do at the turn of the century—made a mathematical prediction of how all the storm's complex relationships would affect its behavior.

Of all the attempts, five programs survived operational tests with enough success to remain in use. Ironically, one consistently useful program ignored all the complex meteorological and theoretical information and required only four pieces of information to make its projection—the current position of the hurricane, its course and speed during the preceding 12 hours, and the date. The computer averaged the courses of all past hurricanes with similar behavior at that time of year and presented the average as the probable track of the present storm.

Despite years of development and testing, the computers invariably disagreed with one another and presented the responsible forecaster with a variety of predictions from which to choose. And the electronic machines proved to be just as baffled as human forecasters by the frequent unexpected accelerations and course changes of abnormal hurricanes. They did not, as some had hoped and expected they would, make forecasting perfect. But they did improve it.

As Robert Simpson reflected on 30 years of detective work in the forefront of

As the U.S. Weather Bureau's chief hurricane forecaster from 1935 to 1954, Grady Norton became a legend in his own time for his uncanny ability to predict the paths of the great storms. Although Norton made full use of technological advances, his forecasts often boiled down to a simple matter of an experienced weatherman's intuition.

hurricane research, he found ample reason for satisfaction. "In the 1950s," he recalled, "the average error in a 24-hour forecast of a hurricane track was 125 miles. Twenty-five years later we had reduced that average error to 115 miles. But before you say that doesn't mean much, remember that these are average errors. And the fact is that in the 1950s we would sometimes be off 200 to 300 miles or more; today, an error of that magnitude is unheard of. When you consider what that means in terms of the evacuation of coastal areas and the preparation of cities for a hurricane emergency, you have to admit that that is significant progress." Yet having said that, Simpson returned to the question that still plagues tropical meteorologists: Why is it not possible to make still better forecasts? And he testified to the notion that better forecasts might involve as much art as science when he recalled a famed meteorologist by the name of Grady Norton.

The legendary Norton had become a weatherman after college in 1915 and had been assigned to take charge of the Hurricane Forecast Center in Jacksonville, Florida, at its inception in 1935. Norton soon proved himself the right man for the job; he had an uncanny knack for predicting the twists and turns of hurricanes, and where they would come ashore in their destructive fury. For 20 years his forecasts, broadcast over a score of radio stations up and down the Gulf and Atlantic coasts of Florida, guided untold thousands of frightened people. So insistent was the public's demand to know what he thought that he stayed on the job long after being advised by doctors to slow down, and he died in 1954 while tracking the approach of Hurricane Hazel.

Simpson remembered Norton best for a forecast he made in 1944 while the forecast center was tracking a storm that showed every sign of bypassing Florida to the south and proceeding westward into the Gulf of Mexico. Simpson was then a hurricane forecaster at the center, and he recalled his surprise at being advised by Norton that the hurricane would not only make a sudden turn northward but would hit land at Tampa Bay 48 hours later.

It happened just that way, and when the storm had passed and the crisis was over, Simpson went to Norton. "I knew everything about that hurricane that you knew," Simpson told him, "and you owe it to me to explain how on earth you arrived at that forecast."

Norton's response was to turn toward a set of glass doors that led onto a 19th-floor penthouse deck outside his office. "When I'm not sure about the way things are going," he explained, "I go out there, sit down, put my feet on the parapet and look out over the everglades. I watch the clouds and ask my question. Usually, the answer comes to me." Ω

GUARDING AGAINST TYPHOONS IN OSAKA

Located on the Yodo River delta at the head of Osaka Bay, the port city of Osaka has been the economic heart of western Japan since the 1500s. But the booming city, known as the Venice of the Orient for its many waterways, is vulnerable to typhoons that sweep in from the Pacific every year.

The bay itself opens to the southwest, directly in line with the track the typhoons usually take from their spawning grounds in the western Pacific. Osaka Bay is also wider, shallower and more gently sloping than the bays of other typhoon-threatened cities, such as nearby Nagoya and Tokyo. Osaka is thus prey to frightful storm surges—huge mounds of water that rise high above sea level as a typhoon comes ashore. Two other factors make Osaka's position even more precarious: The Yodo River system is easily flooded; and because of excessive pumping out of groundwater, most of Osaka's foundation has sunk below sea level, a condition known as subsidence.

In 1961 flooding rains and a storm surge from Typhoon Muroto II killed 32 people and ravaged the city's residential and commercial districts. It was the sixth time in 30 years that Osaka had been swamped, and the city fathers took drastic action.

To halt subsidence, the use of groundwater by industry was restricted. Then, engineers designed an ingenious system of floodgates and pumping stations to block out the storm surges and redirect floodwaters. At last, in 1981, after 16 years of work and the expenditure of $560 million, the entire massive complex—130 miles of embankments, 80 pumping stations and 33 barriers—was in place and ready for battle with the worst a typhoon could offer.

The Tosabori River flows through Osaka in the center of the crowded business district. In the inset above, the same river is seen in full flood, after torrential typhoon rains and a storm surge 13 feet high roared into the port city during Typhoon Muroto II in September of 1961.

A tidal gate, one of five such barriers in Osaka's frontline defense against storm surges, spans the mouth of the Shirinashi River where it opens into the bay. As seen in the cutaway diagram, the arch-shaped barrier is lowered to the bed of the river and forms a dam against flooding; from first warning to final seal takes but 30 minutes. In the open position, the 80-foot arch is high enough for two 800-ton ships to pass beneath it at once.

An electrically operated barrier, one of 28 such devices that control flooding on Osaka's small rivers and canals, stands guard at the Kansaki River, a distributary of the Yodo. As diagramed in the cutaway, the gates fall vertically into place on the riverbed, closing off channels that are ordinarily used for tugboats and barges.

The Sangenya Barrier protects a docking area off the Kizu River, where large seagoing freighters drop anchor. To give the ships clearance, the floodgate is stored beside the barrier in two sections; when high tides endanger the city, the floodgate is carried into blocking position by a giant arm, which extends horizontally over the river and then drops the gate into place.

Inland floods from typhoon rains are controlled with the help of pumping stations, such as the Kema (left), which transfers water from inner-city rivers into a steeply embanked drainage channel. The largest of 80 such installations, the Kema station houses six giant pumps with a total capacity of 67,320 gallons of water per second.

This diagram of the heart of the Osaka typhoon defense system shows how the key components work in concert to prevent flooding from rivers and storm surges. Five arch and sliding tidal gates are in blocking position to keep the raging seas out of a like number of rivers. Meanwhile, inland floodwaters flow into the Okawa, where the Kema Pumping Station transfers the excess into the New Yodo River for drainage into the Pacific.

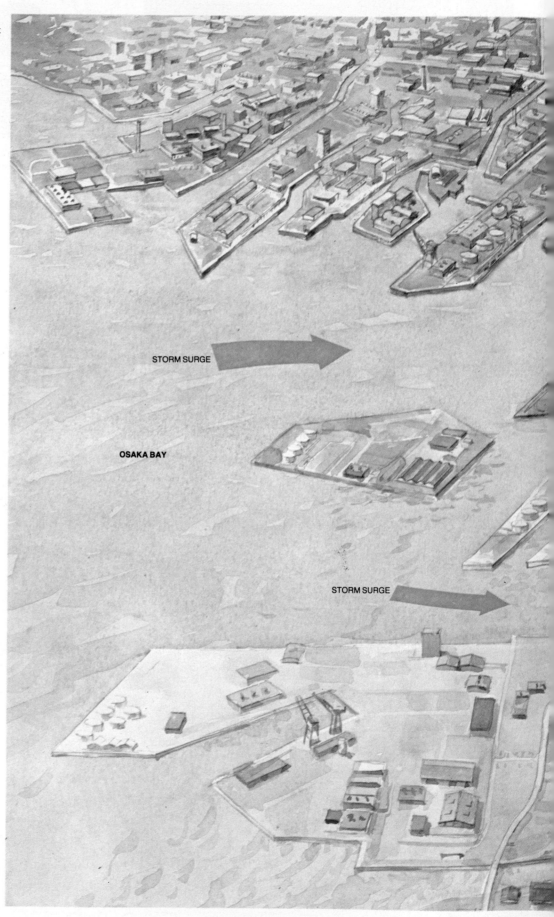

STORM SURGE

OSAKA BAY

STORM SURGE

New Yodo River

KEMA PUMPING
STATION

OSAKA BUSINESS DISTRICT

Okawa

SHORENJI BARRIER

ROKKENYA BARRIER

Tosabori River

INLAND
FLOODWATERS

AJI BARRIER

SHIRINASHI BARRIER

KIZU BARRIER

STORM SURGE

Chapter 5

THUNDERSTORMS AND THEIR PROGENY

Country clerk John M. Bennett of Viroqua, Wisconsin, was a keen weather watcher. On the morning of June 28, 1865, while driving his horse and buggy home after a business trip, Bennett made mental notes that he later entered into his diary: "At sunrise, dark low clouds passing briskly. Cooler. A stiff breeze from the south. Soon reached the valley below and found it warmer (the reverse of the usual condition at this season). At 8 o'clock felt the damp breeze again. Heat increasing. Some cumulus clouds appear. At noon, sultry heat. More cumulus clouds appear. My horse sweating profusely, drove on the walk, and arrived at Viroqua at 1 p.m."

What Bennett had seen and felt was the gathering of elements that would, before the day was done, very nearly cost him his life. By about 3 p.m., as Bennett later recalled, the air was so muggy that "we felt as if we were in the very rain clouds." At about 3:45 streaks of lightning and the crash of thunder signaled a storm two or three miles to the northwest of Viroqua, and another shower was visible to the southeast. Then, wrote Bennett, directly to the west there appeared "a dark, ragged cloud passing swiftly south, and another going north at the same time. On looking at one of them it appeared to stop and go the other way. We had never seen a tornado, but we now knew these clouds were moving swiftly in a circle."

Bennett was torn between fascination and the urge to flee. Curiosity won, and he remained transfixed in his garden while the deadly cloud developed. "The top of the cloud as seen three miles away was only 7° or 8° above the horizon," he reported. "The bottom was on the ground. The motion of this cloud was so rapid that the time of its revolution or rotation was but two or three seconds, and its onward rush was nearly a mile in a minute."

Just west of Viroqua—and squarely in the path of the twister—lay a scoop-shaped basin, about a half mile wide, bordered by rocky hills as high as 60 feet. "Before this cloud reached Viroqua," wrote Bennett, "it had been accompanied by a branch whirl, holding on like a parasite. All of this whirling mass of clouds, now gathered in this low basin, formed a dense cloud 80 rods in diameter horizontally, and about 200 feet deep from bottom to top."

In the basin, the menacing gyre appeared to pause, apparently blocked by the rocky rim. Then "the upper and wider portions overflowed the barriers and in this disturbed condition took the form of branches of the main portion and here and there reached down and destroyed any building in their way."

Among the first to be demolished was a large new warehouse, sturdily constructed of heavy timbers, owned by one Herman Greve and used to store farm machinery and produce—including on this day a bulky pile of unsacked fleece.

Heralding the approach of a midafternoon thunderstorm, black scud clouds whipped by gusty downdrafts cast an eerie pall over a desert road in southwest Arizona. Sheets of rain that were beginning to fall when this photo was snapped drenched the parched landscape in just half an hour.

The structure was instantly ripped apart, its massive timbers lifted 50 feet or more into the air and then "dashed down upon the rocks around, causing a jarring of the ground many rods away."

At that belated point Bennett, his wife, their grown daughter and six-year-old granddaughter "went with all haste to the cellar with death in view, as we thought." Mrs. Bennett, narrowly avoiding a falling chimney, was the last of the four to reach the refuge, where she fell on her knees, crying: "Lord save or we perish!"

The Bennetts' home was shattered and Bennett himself was pinned beneath fallen timbers, his right leg broken just above the ankle. His cap and the women's hair nets and even hairpins were snatched away by the clawing wind. "The hair of our heads in a whirl," wrote Bennett, "we were for one dreadful minute pierced with flying splinters, our eyes and hair filled with mingled street dust and pulverized plastering, mixed with blood flowing from our bleeding scalps."

These contemporary engravings depict the havoc visited by a tornado on Viroqua, Wisconsin, on June 28, 1865. The twister cut a broad swath through the town and the neighboring countryside (*left*), killing more than a score of people and demolishing 80 buildings, including the Methodist Church (*above, top*) and the local newspaper printing office (*above, bottom*).

Bennett's horse had been stabled about 50 feet east of the house. The 1,100-pound animal was picked up as if it were a toy and "dropped from the whirl directly upon us. His head was by the side of mine so I could breathe in his face. He was held here in his struggles by timbers around him."

The satanic swirl passed as swiftly as it had come—and, as an eerie quiet fell over the wreckage of his home, John Bennett fainted.

But the dervish was by no means done. In its several whirling winds it killed 17 persons in Viroqua. Then the segments converged into a single column that roared out of town toward the east—where, two miles away on open prairie, stood a schoolhouse with 24 pupils. By the time help arrived, five children were dead and a sixth, mortally injured, lay cradled in the lap of her teacher, who was herself gravely hurt.

Reaching the West Kickapoo River, the twister rose over 400-foot bluffs and, no longer touching the ground, shifted course to the northeast. It was last seen sometime after 4 p.m., 30 miles from Viroqua, in the form of an ugly black cloud from which were falling, as if in an unseasonable snow, tufts of fleece from Herman Greve's warehouse.

Tornadoes such as Viroqua's killing cloud carry within their deadly coils the most violent of all the winds that sweep the world. Twisters exist but for a gasp of time—most typically less than 20 minutes and rarely more than two or three hours. On the earth's vast surface, tornadoes trace minikin tracks, usually no more than a quarter of a mile wide or 15 miles long. In the United States, only .5 per cent of all tornadoes traverse more than 100 miles (but those few superstorms account for almost 20 per cent of the nation's tornado deaths).

No region on the planet is entirely safe from tornadoes. The British Isles, for example, average about 60 a year; although exact figures are not available for the

European continent, during a recent 25-year period an annual average of 10 tornadoes was reported in Italy. Australia reports an average of 14.6 per year, but this figure may be low because of the sparseness of the population. Tornadoes on the African continent are rare, and in India the few that have been reported have occurred in one small area, at the northern end of the Bay of Bengal.

In the raw number and savagery of its tornadoes, the United States is without peer. During a recent span of three decades, no fewer than 19,312 tornadoes—more than 640 a year—were reported in the continental United States. During the peak month of May each year, an average of five tornadoes a day unleashed their insensate fury upon the land. Over the last 50 years tornadoes in the United States have killed some 9,000 persons—a number equal to the combined total of lives taken by floods (5,000) and hurricanes (4,000); between 1970 and 1976 annual property damage averaged about $300 million.

So vicious are tornadoes, and so frequently freakish are they in their behavior, that they sometimes seem to have an existence entirely their own, independent of other natural forces. In fact, however, a tornado is no more than a spectacular sibling in the family of severe local storms. Among such atmospheric tumults, the most familiar by far is the thunderstorm, and it is the glowering thunderstorm that is associated with the vast majority of tornadoes.

During the course of each year, more than 16 million thunderstorms—an average of 45,000 a day—maul the face of the earth. At any given moment, some 2,000 are in simultaneous progress, drenching the planet with water, buffeting its occupants with high winds, illuminating its skies with lethal lightning and often pounding its surface with hailstones.

Although man has lived with thunderstorms since the dawn of his day on earth, knowledge of their genesis and their internal mechanisms remains imperfect. Still, as meteorologists strive for greater understanding of severe local storms, their quest takes them ever deeper into the veiled, violent world of the cumulonimbus clouds wherein are generated forces beyond belief.

In its least complex and perhaps most commonplace form, the thunderstorm cumulonimbus appears as a lonely giant, black and brooding in the sky. As wide as 50 miles at its base, the isolated cloud may tower 10 or more miles high, reaching into the tropopause—the border between the troposphere and the stratosphere—where horizontal winds and lower temperatures flatten and distend its crown into a characteristic anvil shape.

Within that gloomy mass churn energies equal to 10 or more Hiroshima-type nuclear bombs. Yet thunderstorm formation begins unseen and unheard, on relatively small tracts of earth basking in the heat of the sun. A primary ingredient in thunderstorm development is differential, or uneven, heating. A hilltop, for example, may receive the sun's rays more directly than the flatter areas nearby; similarly, air in contact with land heats more rapidly than air above bodies of water. At any rate, warm air amid cooler air begins to rise, almost as if it were a bubble—and the higher it goes, the more hostile the environment it encounters.

As the bubble reaches a low-level layer of cool, dry air, the vapor within it condenses into droplets of water, forming harmless little white cumulus clouds, dozens of which may be scattered across the skyscape like grazing sheep. These first cumulus clouds, lying at a height of from 2,000 to 5,000 feet, are short-lived; dry, cool air causes evaporation and cooling. But in turn, rapid evaporation adds moisture to the air around the clouds, thereby ensuring that succeeding clouds will dwell in a friendlier climate. As the process continues, new clouds last longer and grow taller than those that have dissipated; several may merge into a single, much larger cloud whose outer portions act as insulation for the heated air still rising within.

Eventually, however, even the protected updraft reaches an altitude so cold that its vapor particles begin to freeze. The weight of these moisture particles becomes too great for the updraft to sustain, and with the cumulonimbus in this highly unstable condition, an overturning occurs. Even as warm air continues to rush upward at speeds as great as 60 miles per hour, pellets of ice or drops of water begin to descend. By their drag they create downdrafts; when the downdrafts near the earth, they spread horizontally and become manifest as the strong gusts of wind that invariably precede a thunderstorm.

Within an isolated cumulonimbus, several separate updrafts and an equal number of downdrafts may exist simultaneously; each updraft-downdraft couple is known as a cell, and as many as five cells often occur within a single cumulonimbus. Such cells are of brief duration, rarely more than 20 minutes, partly because they produce deluges of water that cool the earth and tend to choke the warm updrafts at their source. But as a cumulonimbus proceeds on its wind-wafted course above the land, new cells may replace old ones, and a thunderstorm may last several hours.

In textbook terms, the birth-to-death evolution of a thunderstorm is predictable and orderly, a measured progression of events. Yet the books give no sugges-

With tornadoes brewing in its swirling mass, the leading edge of an unusually powerful thunderstorm, called a supercell because its life cycle is many times longer than most tornadic storms, advances eastward over central Kansas. The giant storm dumped five inches of rain on the area and spawned more than six funnels (tornadoes that do not touch ground) and one actual tornado that damaged six farms.

tion of the nightmare demons that dwell within the majestic cumulonimbus. So terrible are the shearing updrafts and downdrafts, so drowning the rains, that not even the most modern aircraft can enter the dark towers with impunity. Many a pilot has gone to his doom in a thunderhead. One flier who experienced the furies and lived to tell about it was a U.S. Marine Corps fighter pilot who spent more than half an hour, alone and dangling helplessly from a parachute's slender shrouds, at the mercy of the maelstrom.

For Lieutenant Colonel William H. Rankin, a decorated veteran of World War II and the Korean War, the sunny Sunday of July 26, 1959, promised to be routine in every respect. He was scheduled to make a simple 600-mile navigational flight from South Weymouth, Massachusetts, to Beaufort, North Carolina, in his F8U Crusader jet fighter. Just before his late-afternoon departure he checked with the meteorologist at the Massachusetts air station and was told that he might run into thunderstorms, with cloudtops at 30,000 to 40,000 feet, around Norfolk, Virginia. The forecast was nothing to worry an experienced pilot. "Well," said Rankin, "I'll go to 50,000 feet and get over the weather."

Nearing Norfolk at about 6 p.m., Rankin saw the black and roiling mass of a thunderstorm, its tops slightly higher than the predicted 40,000 feet. Then, as he climbed to 47,000 feet, Rankin heard a thump and a rumbling sound within his plane; the bright red fire-warning light flashed on, and the aircraft rapidly lost power. Examination of the wreckage later disclosed that the plane had suffered an engine seizure, caused by extreme friction of unknown cause. Some 20 seconds after he had first heard the ominous noises, while he was still at 47,000 feet, Rankin ejected.

"I had never heard of anyone's having ejected at this altitude," he wrote later. "The temperature outside was close to 70° below zero. I had on only a summer-weight flying suit, gloves, helmet and marine field shoes." As he hurtled through the air, Rankin almost instantly felt an intense stinging sensation that quickly turned to "a blessed numbness." At the same time, the sudden change from the controlled atmosphere of the cockpit to the rarified upper air caused an agonizing decompression. "I could feel my abdomen distending, stretching, until I thought it would burst," he recalled. "My eyes felt as though they were being ripped from their sockets, my head as if it were splitting into several parts, my ears bursting inside, my entire body racked by cramps."

Surprisingly, Rankin's free fall into the thundercloud brought relief. His parachute, equipped with a barometric sensing device, was designed to open automatically at 10,000 feet. The denser air eased both the cold and the pain of decompression—and even as he plummeted at a rate of 10,000 feet per minute, Rankin had enough left of his senses to glance at his wrist watch. He had ejected at exactly 6 o'clock, and although it was difficult to see in the dense clouds, the luminous hands of the watch now seemed to indicate about 6:05. A few seconds later, Rankin's chute opened.

Assuming that he was now at 10,000 feet and calculating that he would require about 10 relatively tranquil minutes to reach the ground, Rankin began to relax. In fact, his awful ride had only begun—the parachute's triggering sensor had evidently been fooled by the barometric pressure within the cloud—and Rankin was about to enter the heart of the storm.

"A massive blast of air jarred me from head to toe," he recalled. "I went soaring up and up and up. Falling again, I saw that I was in an angry ocean of boiling clouds—blacks and grays and whites, spilling over one another, into one another, digesting one another.

"I became a molecule trapped in the thermal pattern of the heat engine, buffeted in all directions—up, down, sideways, clockwise, counterclockwise, over and over. I zoomed straight up, straight down, feeling all the weird sensations of G forces—positive, negative and zero. I was stretched, slammed and pounded. I was a bag of flesh and bones crashing into a concrete floor.

"At one point, after I had been shot up like a shell leaving a cannon, I found myself looking down into a long, black tunnel. Sometimes, not wanting to see what was going on, I shut my eyes. This was nature's bedlam, a black cageful of screaming lunatics, beating me with big flat sticks, roaring at me, trying to crush me. All this time it had been raining so torrentially that I thought I would drown in mid-air. Several times I had held my breath, fearing to inhale quarts of water."

At last, Rankin sensed that the turbulence was diminishing. Opening his eyes, he took a quick look—and saw beneath him a patch of green earth. Minutes later—after smashing into the trunk of a tree—he came to ground. The time was 6:40 p.m.

After his frightful experience, pilot Rankin was much the worse for wear: His body was covered with bruises and lacerations; during decompression his torso had swelled so much that it now bore imprints from the stitched seams of his flying suit; ligaments, joints and muscles were strained and sprained; he suffered temporary amnesia and loss of equilibrium. But he recovered rapidly and was

Borne aloft by the convection currents within a thunderstorm's cumulus cloud, a hailstone nucleus rises and falls repeatedly as it collects supercooled water droplets. The stone's trajectory has been simplified in the diagram; in fact, a growing hailstone can undergo any number of ascents and descents—and may even leave and reenter the cloud—before falling to the ground.

For its sudden destruction of crops, farmers call hail the "white plague." "It wipes you out in the passing of a cloud," complained a Colorado farm boy bitterly. "Half an hour ago you had a half-section of wheat—320 acres—ready to harvest and haul to town. Now you haven't got a penny."

Thousands of hailstorms occur each year, especially in the moist, temperate climates of the middle latitudes. In the United States alone, crop damage from hail totals about one billion dollars a year, with a further $75 million in losses attributable to livestock deaths and property damage.

The groundwork for such devastation is laid innocently enough, deep within a thunderstorm's cumulus cloud. There, at frigid altitudes above 15,000 feet, the air is at first so pure that water droplets can exist at temperatures well below the freezing point without turning to ice.

As the storm's convection currents become more powerful, however, they sweep tiny particles of dust and ice upward into the cloud. Each of these foreign bodies —a potential hailstone nucleus—begins to collide with supercooled water droplets, which freeze to it on impact. Buffeted about by a series of updrafts and downdrafts, the hailstone gathers layer upon layer of ice. When it has grown so heavy that even the strongest updraft cannot sustain it, the mature hailstone plummets to earth.

While weak storms produce small stones that melt before reaching the ground, severe thunderstorms are capable of generating hail the size of eggs, baseballs or even grapefruit. When a particularly violent storm ravaged Coffeyville, Kansas, on September 3, 1970, residents collected scores of unusually large hailstones, including one that measured nearly six inches in diameter and weighed 1⅔ pounds (far left, bottom). When the amazing specimen was sent to Colorado's National Center for Atmospheric Research, meteorologists confirmed that it set a new record for size—and calculated that, in its final stages of growth, the stone had required an updraft of 100 miles per hour to keep it in the air.

Reflecting a myriad of colors when viewed under polarized light, a thin cross section of the largest hailstone on record (shown here at one third its actual size) exhibits hail's crystalline structure and concentric rings. The irregular knobs were caused by water flowing upward as the stone fell.

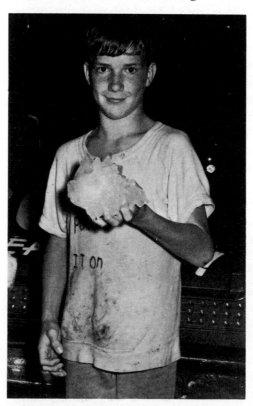

A Coffeyville, Kansas, youth displays a giant hailstone he found in his yard during the September 1970 storm. He wore a football helmet for protection against the potentially lethal missiles.

Looking as though it had been subjected to an antiaircraft barrage, a DC-6 airliner bears witness to the destructive power of hail. Fear of such damage helped to convince airlines in the 1950s that they should equip their planes with radar.

A canopy of mammatus clouds overhangs the Kansas countryside at sunset on June 6, 1971. Such pendulous cloud formations developing beneath the anvil-shaped tops of thunderstorms frequently presage tornadoes; in this case they accompanied a storm system that produced a total of 37 twisters in Kansas, Nebraska, Iowa and Missouri.

soon flying again. To the end of his days, however, he would surely carry with him the memory of those minutes within what meteorologists routinely describe as an "isolated thunderstorm."

For all its convulsive power, Rankin's thunderstorm was but a solitary, relatively harmless member of a family that—as far as man's meteorological awareness is concerned—is still growing. Only recently recognized, for example, are giant thunderstorm combinations that have been given the cumbersome name of Mesoscale Convective Complexes.

In the formation of such a complex, several individual thunderstorms are brought together by some as yet unknown attraction into a single, highly organized system covering upward of 40,000 square miles and lasting 12 hours or longer. But these mesoscale systems do not act simply like overgrown versions of ordinary thunderstorms. Says meteorologist J. Michael Fritsch, who has been studying the phenomenon under the auspices of the National Oceanic and Atmospheric Administration in Boulder, Colorado: "In terms of the structure of their winds, the source of energy, the way atmospheric circulation is affected and the internal cloud structure, they are put together and behave differently than any other system." Mesoscale Convective Complexes differ from ordinary squall lines in their shape, their size and in when they occur; they are for the most part summertime storms, with little or no upper-level wind to push them along.

"And, more surprising," adds Fritsch, "they are all over the damn place." In the American Midwest, where the mesoscale complexes are particularly prevalent, between 60 and 100 may occur each year. They are usually characterized by steady heavy rains and thus are a blessing to farmers. They may also be a boon to meteorologists: Because of their great size and relatively long duration, they lend themselves to study and could therefore provide valuable clues about the physics of other convective systems—including the squall lines that are among the most destructive members of the thunderstorm family.

Squall lines are primarily spawned by differential advection. As opposed to the vertical airflow of convection, advection is the transport by horizontal winds of cold air over warm air or dry air over moist air. And again the American Midwest, where warm air pushed northward from the Gulf of Mexico is frequent-

124

ly overridden by westerly cold air from the Rocky Mountains, offers an ideal incubator. Usually present between the warm and cold masses is a layer of comparatively stable air, in which the temperature, rather than decreasing with height, may actually increase. This inversion, as it is called, acts as a sort of shield between the contrasting masses, preventing the warm air from rising into the colder levels.

But as the sun heats the ground, pockets of especially warm air may develop and force their way through the inversion barrier, forming strong thunderstorm cells strung out on a line many miles long. In its mature form a squall line is unmistakable as it scuds or rolls and tumbles across the countryside, the base of its clouds whipped and shredded by wind. The two kinds of clouds that characterize a squall line are puffy, cylindrical roll clouds and flatter shelf clouds with clearly defined upper edges and ragged bases.

Sailors have always regarded squall lines as among the most fearsome of natural hazards. And numerous fliers, before the day of all-seeing radar, came to grief attempting to pick a course through the squall line's deadly clumps of thunderstorm cells. In fact, it was just such a storm system that brought disaster to one of America's more ambitious endeavors in flight.

The sleek silver airship christened *Shenandoah* was a direct descendent of the German Zeppelins that had raided London during World War I. The United States Navy envisioned airships as far-ranging scouts for its Pacific fleet. They would be safe to fly: Whereas the German dirigibles had been filled with highly flammable hydrogen, the American craft would be inflated with nonflammable helium, a rare lifting gas found only in Texas and Kansas.

The *Shenandoah* was built by the Navy at a cost of three million dollars and on September 4, 1923, it cast off for its maiden flight from an abandoned Army camp in the piny woods near Lakehurst, New Jersey. A voyage of exploration to the North Pole was scheduled, but it was canceled by President Calvin Coolidge on grounds of economics; it would be too expensive and too risky, he judged. The airship did, however, make a 1925 round trip between Lakehurst and the West Coast, spending 235 hours in the air—and inspiring dreams that craft of the *Shenandoah* type could provide the United States with its first transcontinental air passenger service.

Sailing through the sky, the *Shenandoah* was a splendid sight—680.25 feet long, 78.7 feet in diameter, designed to carry 2,115,174 cubic feet of helium

Dark with menace, a squall line advances across the Chesapeake Bay in Virginia on a summer afternoon in 1977. The thunderstorms that make up a squall line, with their torrential rains and shifting winds, can be extremely perilous to small craft caught in open water.

and driven by six Packard engines, each rated at 300 horsepower. Wherever the airship went, traffic stopped on the streets below and throngs gathered to witness the spectacle. The U.S. Navy knew a good public relations device when it saw one, and for early September, 1925, the service slated a trip from Lakehurst to Detroit, during which the ship would appear over several state fairs. It would be the *Shenandoah's* 57th flight.

At 2:52 p.m. on September 2, the airship rose from the 160-foot Lakehurst mooring mast, steering westward. The skipper was Lieutenant Commander Zachary Lansdowne, 36, who had, as an observer aboard the British R 34 in 1919, become the first American to fly from England to the United States in a rigid airship. As fate would have it, Lansdowne was writing a manual in which, among other things, he warned that rigid airships should, at all costs and whether filled with helium or hydrogen, avoid thunderstorms.

In the early-morning darkness of September 3, lightning flashes to the north and east signaled the lurking presence of thunderstorms. Following his own advice, Lansdowne ordered a change of course toward the south, where the sky seemed to be clear. But near Ava, Ohio, at about 4:30 a.m., there suddenly appeared off the *Shenandoah's* starboard bow a long, dark, streaky, fast-moving cloud bank—a typical squall line.

Almost instantly, the *Shenandoah* was seized by the frenzy of the storm. "The ship is rising a meter a second, Captain!" reported the elevator man in the control car. Despite desperate efforts to check the ascent, the big ship soared from 1,600 to 3,000 feet. There, pitching violently, it paused briefly—and then started up again, this time at a rate of nearly 1,000 feet per minute. At 6,000 feet, the ascent halted almost as abruptly as it had begun. Now the *Shenandoah* began to plunge through the sky. Having already released helium to check the climb, crewmen frantically began to jettison water ballast to stop the

Torn loose by the updrafts and downdrafts of a wide area of thunderstorms on September 3, 1925, the stern of the U.S. Navy airship *Shenandoah* lies in tangled ruin on a hill in eastern Ohio. The crash led to changes in the design of later ships, but cast an indelible shadow on the already troubled future of the giant airborne liners.

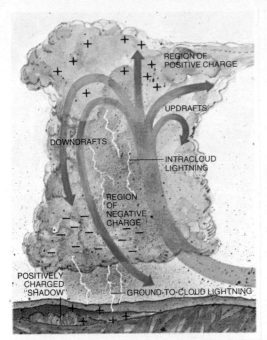

Lightning occurs when a thundercloud becomes polarized. According to one theory, updrafts carry light, positively charged ice particles into upper cloud regions while downdrafts speed the descent of heavy, negatively charged water droplets. These negative ions then repel electrons from the earth, inducing a positive "shadow" under the cloud. When the charge differentials become excessive, an electrical current—lightning—flows between regions of opposite charge, both in the cloud and between cloud and ground.

fall. At 3,000 feet another updraft caught the helpless *Shenandoah*. Spinning crazily, with its bow pointed upward at an angle of nearly 30 degrees, the ship began to rise again. Then it broke in two.

In the control car, Lansdowne heard the banshee shriek of tearing metal and said calmly: "Anyone who wants to leave the car may do so." Two men clambered up a ladder into the forward hull section; Lansdowne and seven others remained. Until now, the broken sections of the airship had been attached to each other by the heavy rudder and elevator cables leading from the control car to the tail. But the cables soon gave way—and the control car plummeted to earth, killing all its occupants. Moments later the two forward-engine gondolas and the radio car broke loose, carrying six men to their death. Astonishingly, 29 men survived, floating to the ground in bits and pieces of the airship whose cells had retained part of their helium.

In the inquiry that followed, a Navy board attributed the destruction of the *Shenandoah* to "large, unbalanced, external aerodynamic forces arising from high velocity air currents." Had the *Shenandoah* been inflated with hydrogen, all hands would surely have perished in explosions triggered by the lightning within the squall line.

Wherever thunderstorms occur, and of whatever size or sort they may be, there too is lightning, with its noisy companion, thunder. Among all weather phenomena, lightning is perhaps the foremost killer: Although statistics are inexact, as many as 200 persons a year may die as lightning victims in the United States alone. The heat of a single lightning flash is intense beyond imagining: Within millionths of a second the temperature may reach 50,000° F., almost five times that of the sun's surface. And the amount of electrical energy expended by lightning is staggering: It has been estimated that lightning strikes about 100 times per second around the circumference of the globe—a rate of discharge that represents about four billion kilowatts of continuous power.

Yet for all its lethal ubiquity, lightning in many respects remains a puzzle to scientists. Lightning is defined as the visible electrical emission from a charged cloud. It is known that the upper regions of thunderclouds are positively charged while the lower portions contain negative charges; the cloud thus acts as an enormous electrostatic machine.

But how does the cloud become electrified in the first place? No one, alas, really knows. A widely held theory is that when a cloud's temperature approaches the freezing point, droplets of negatively charged water are surrounded by tiny particles of positively charged ice. The updraft-downdraft turbulence within the cloud sorts out the water, which then descends, from the lighter weight ice crystals, which are borne aloft. At any event, immense electrical stresses, capable of generating as many as 100 million volts, are rapidly built up between the opposing poles. Eventually the charge becomes so great that it overwhelms the capacity of air to act as an insulator, and lightning may ensue either entirely within a cloud or along horizontal lines between clouds.

At the same time, although the earth is ordinarily negatively charged, a positive reaction is caused by the negative particles in the base of a cloud passing overhead. Therefore, as a thundercloud drifts through the sky it is followed on earth by what has been described as a positively charged "electrical shadow," which climbs all obstacles—hills, chimneys, towers, steeples—in its path. The higher it rises, the more likely it is to establish a flow of current between itself and the cloud.

That flow, of course, is a lightning stroke. It begins when a faint electrical impulse, known as a step leader, courses downward from the cloud. The step leader streaks down for 100 feet or more, pauses, then continues in a sequence that might be compared to separate pulses of an electrical current.

By this process, which requires about 1/100 second, a conductive channel,

Splitting the sky with fierce traceries, lightning
imparts a surreal glow to the Kitt Peak National
Observatory in Sells, Arizona. Although the
luminous path of each flash is only an inch or two in
diameter, the bolts at far left and far right appear
much broader than the others because they struck
closer to the camera, overexposing its film.

perhaps no wider than a pencil but as long as five miles, is established. As the channel nears the ground, the positively charged shadow itself sends up streamers, usually from the highest protuberance on its surface. When these streamers make contact with the descending step leader, a circuit is completed and a white-hot return stroke surges skyward traveling at hundreds of millions of feet per second along the conductive channel already created.

That return stroke, and the glow of the superheated air for several feet around its thin channel, constitutes the lightning flash so familiar and so frightening to humankind. And despite the false evidence provided by man's eye, it leaps not from the sky to the earth but from ground to cloud. As for thunder, it is nothing more than the sound given off by the rapid heating and expansion of gases within the lightning channel.

In its effects, the power of lightning is awesome, and frequently freakish. It has been known to reduce the wooden masts of sailing ships to shavings that littered the sea; it has melted holes in church bells, welded chains into iron bars and even cooked potatoes in their fields. In the United States, some 10,000 forest fires a year are attributed to lightning. On occasion lightning strikes a grounded human directly, but most deaths and injuries are caused by side flashes from nearby elevated objects, such as trees, or by the high voltage in the earth around a spot that has been hit by lightning. The steel shaft of a club raised during a golfer's backswing is particularly attractive to lightning, as is an umbrella or a portable-radio antenna. Using a telephone during a thunderstorm can be fatal if lightning happens to strike a nearby utility pole and travel along the wires.

Strangely, humans who enter lightning's own element, the air, are generally safer than those who remain on earth. Although hydrogen-filled rigid airships were susceptible to lightning damage because of their fabric covering and the highly volatile gas, modern metal aircraft are largely invulnerable. Instead of penetrating a plane, lightning's electrical current merely flows through its structure, usually leaving nothing more than a few pit marks as evidence of its presence.

Still, there are exceptions. In 1938, for example, the pilot of a British airliner flying through a dark nimbostratus rain cloud over Toulouse, France, opened his cockpit window for better visibility. A fiery ball of lightning —an unusual phenomenon that scientists have not as yet been able to explain— danced through the window, singed off the pilot's eyebrows and rolled through the forward passenger cabin into the rear compartment, where it exploded noisily but harmlessly.

Lightning in aircraft is not always so ineffective. On December 8, 1963, a bolt struck a Pan American World Airways 707 jetliner over Elkton, Maryland, with catastrophic results. The lightning penetrated a reserve fuel tank in the wing, igniting the vapors and sending the 707 plummeting in a ball of fire. Eighty-two passengers and crew died in the crash.

The Elkton disaster was one of the few instances where lightning has been accused as a mass killer. In the doleful catalogue of thunderstorm manifestations, that role has been played mainly by the tornado.

Cutting from south to north across the flat central plains of the United States is a slice of land 460 miles in length and 400 miles in width. This is the swath known as Tornado Alley, extending from northern Texas through Oklahoma, Kansas and Missouri, where as many as 300 tornadoes touch down each year, more by far than any place else on earth. The same conditions that are conducive to massive thunderstorms in the area—warm moist air from the Gulf of Mexico colliding with cooler dry air masses sweeping across from the west—are responsible for the stupendous number of tornadoes. So frequent are the whirlwinds there that most farmers and many townspeople build their homes with cyclone

Captured in a remarkable sequence of photographs, a twister that touched down near Osnabrock, North Dakota, on July 6, 1978, shows a classic pattern of tornado development. A white funnel of condensation—a rapidly spinning cloud—has descended to earth from a severe thunderstorm. As it moves along the ground, suction and rotating winds pick up dirt and debris, surrounding the tornado with a sleeve of dust. Toward the end of the sequence the funnel narrows and loses power; the dust diminishes as the funnel commences its retreat back up into the well-defined collar cloud above it.

A multiple-vortex tornado churns on the eastern edge of Wichita Falls, Texas, after grinding through the city on April 10, 1979. Six suction vortices—minitwisters of extreme violence—orbit the tornado's center in various stages of maturity (*diagram above*). The monstrous storm killed 44 people and demolished nearly 8,000 homes.

cellars, sturdy underground shelters to which they and their families can flee when the twisters come howling down out of the sky.

On the sullen, sultry afternoon of June 22, 1928, a Kansas farmer named Will Keller was tending his fields when he saw, coming fast, the twisting tentacle of a tornado. Calling to his family, Keller ran to his cyclone cellar. Just as he was about to slam the door against the oncoming monster, some impulse prompted him to turn for a last glance: "As I paused to look I saw that the lower end which had been sweeping the ground was beginning to rise. I knew what that meant, so I kept my position. I knew that I was comparatively safe and I knew that if the tornado again dipped I could drop down and close the door before any harm could be done.

"Steadily the tornado came on, the end gradually rising above the ground. I could have stood there only a few seconds but so impressed was I with what was going on that it seemed a long time. At last the great shaggy end of the funnel hung directly overhead.

"Everything was as still as death. There was a strong gassy odor and it seemed that I could not breathe. There was a screaming, hissing sound coming directly from the end of the funnel. I looked up and to my astonishment I saw right up into the heart of the tornado.

"There was a circular opening in the center of the funnel, about 50 or 100 feet in diameter, and extending straight upward for a distance of at least one-half mile, as best I could judge under the circumstances. The walls of this opening were of rotating clouds and the whole was made brilliantly visible by constant flashes of lightning which zigzagged from side to side.

"Around the lower rim of the great vortex small tornadoes were constantly forming and breaking away. These looked like tails as they writhed their way around the end of the funnel. It was these that made the hissing noise. I noticed that the direction and rotation of the great whirl was anticlockwise, but the small twisters rotated both ways—some one way and some another."

Will Keller was one of the very few mortals ever to peer into the eye of a tornado and live to tell about it. Indeed, so savage are the winds within a twister that tornadoes through most of meteorological history have defied all efforts to probe their inner mysteries, even with instruments; such devices as anemometers and barometers rarely survive tornadic forces. According to Edwin Kessler, director of the National Severe Storms Laboratory in Norman, Oklahoma, a tornado "is so violent and so ephemeral that until recently it didn't lend itself to study."

The Small Twisters That Spin at Sea

As a rule, winds over water exhibit more power than those over land, where friction and obstruction sap their strength. But the waterspout is an intriguing exception.

Though waterspouts are caused by the same convective processes that spawn tornadoes, they are generally weaker because the sharp temperature differences that underlie the dynamics of tornadoes are not present over the sea. While tornado winds may reach 300 miles per hour, those in a waterspout rarely exceed 50 miles per hour and usually last less than 15 minutes.

Waterspouts occur mainly in shallow coastal waters; around Florida hundreds occur every summer, sometimes two or three at once. But while they can be dangerous to small craft, they rarely do more than give the crews of larger vessels a spectacular few moments. As a waterspout passed over one freighter, the crew reported sharp winds gusting in opposite directions fore and aft, while amidships there was dead calm.

Dwarfing a nearby pier, a waterspout spins in bright sunlight off the coast of Spain near Gerona on September 2, 1965. The whirling force of the vortex whisked sea water at the base of the funnel into a huge misty curtain called a spray ring.

And more is the pity since, as Kessler adds, a tornado is "perhaps the ultimate meteorological phenomenon."

In its most familiar form, a tornado is a funnel-shaped, vaporous mass with winds rotating around a vertical axis at high speeds as it reaches down from a thundercloud or a squall line. The main ingredients necessary to the formation of a tornado are convergence and rotation. Convergence—the coming together of air masses with different temperatures and moisture content—is of course the circumstance that gives rise to thunderstorms. But a tornado requires something to give the convergent elements a spin. Considering the rapid development of tornadoes, the Coriolis effect, by which the earth's motion around its own axis imparts rotation to air masses, probably does not have time to play a decisive part. Instead, it seems more than possible that the rotational impetus is provided when strong lateral winds enter cloud formations and create shear conditions that cause rising columns of warm air to veer and spiral.

The spinning starts slowly, then as the spiral tightens it picks up speed in what is known as the ice skater process: As a rotating figure skater brings her arms in, she spins faster and faster.

Before a tornado appears, strange udder-like protuberances may develop on the underside of a thundercloud anvil. Called mammatus—from the Latin word which means "having breasts"—the clouds are caused by the sinking of moist cold air and furnish grim warning of the turmoil within. However, mammatus clouds do not usually form along squall lines, where the first observable indication of a potential tornado is likely to be rotary circulation in the wind-tattered cloud bases.

Soon after rotation has been established within a cloud, a whirling tendril extends downward, growing larger and larger, longer and longer until it contacts the earth in an explosion of flying dirt and debris. Up to that moment the tornadic cloud has been grayish white; now, sweeping up earthly matter like an enormous vacuum cleaner, it is rapidly darkened by its contents. (As always happens with tornadoes, there are exceptions: A tornado passing over a Utah snowfield in 1970 turned white as driven snow.)

Taking its direction—usually from the southwest toward the northeast—from the parent cloud, the funnel advances at forward speeds that average about 30 miles per hour but may exceed 60; the tornado may bounce and skip, rising briefly from the ground and then touching down again; it sways from side to side, sometimes tilting forward and leaving behind it on the earth semicircular suction marks, which were mistaken by the ancients for the hoofprints of a colossal horse.

With a distinctive yet indescribable roar that can be heard for several miles, the tornado wreaks its ruin not only by the battering power of its whirling winds but by the suction set up within its vortex. Tornadic winds were once thought to reach speeds of more than 700 miles per hour, but more recent estimates indicate maximum velocities of little more than 300 miles an hour. That reduction, however, is small comfort, since the impact of wind increases by the square—a 300-mile-per-hour wind is thus not 10 times but 100 times more damaging than one of 30 miles per hour.

Similarly, it was long believed that the low-pressure region at the core of a tornado caused structures on the ground to explode outward; from that idea grew the notion that windows should be opened upon the approach of a tornado so as to equalize the pressures within and without buildings. But recent studies give evidence that although the pressure inside a tornado may indeed drop by as much as two pounds per square inch, damage to buildings is mainly caused by quite a different phenomenon. In much the same fashion that air flowing at high speed across the curved upper surface of wings provides the uplift that carries an airplane from the ground, so the rush of tornadic winds along a rooftop can literally pluck a house from its foundation. To humans whose lives and property are

Fantastic Pranks by Tornado Winds

Tornadoes have long been famous not only for the devastation they can bring, but also for the freakish tricks that frequently mark their passing. Incredible though these pranks may seem, all are natural effects of the storm's multiple vortices and high-velocity winds.

On April 18, 1955, in Lanark, Illinois, a twister swept up a car containing two people, transported it aloft for 100 feet, and deposited it right side up without injuring the terrified occupants. A tornado once carried an entire house for two miles; another kept a roof airborne for 12 miles. During the infamous Tri-State Tornado that raged through Missouri, Illinois and Indiana on March 18, 1925, high winds ripped a railroad bridge from its foundations.

A tornado's multiple vortices—small, fast-spinning columns of air within the twister itself—often seem to single out individual objects for damage. On April 3, 1974, a family in Madison, Indiana, huddled in a bedroom closet seeking shelter from an approaching funnel cloud. The tornado demolished the rest of the house, but did not touch the closet. Another house was reduced to rubble, but the kitchen cupboard, still full of dishes, was borne aloft. Ascending air currents cushioned its descent and the cupboard eventually settled to earth—with every dish still intact. Through similar acts of selectivity, tornadoes have safely carried a jar of pickles for 25 miles, and have partially defeathered chickens (*opposite*).

Some of the more bizarre effects of a tornado occur when ordinarily harmless objects attain high velocities. A twister that roared through St. Louis, Missouri, in 1896 propelled a pine two-by-four through a solid iron wall ⅝ inch thick. And following a 1951 tornado in Scottsbluff, Nebraska, puzzled residents discovered an otherwise undamaged egg with a single neat hole in its shell. Without so much as cracking the egg, the whimsical twister had shot a bean into the yolk.

A Blue Springs, Nebraska, farmer contemplates a baby grand piano pitched into a field by a September 26, 1973, tornado. The twister's fierce winds carried the 500-pound missile some 1,300 feet, tossing a leather boot onto its sounding board as a final touch of incongruity.

A basketball standard in Monticello, Indiana, bows in obeisance to one of nature's most powerful manifestations. This 1974 tornado also blew in the windows of the school in the background—fortunately, after the students had left for the day.

Mangled almost beyond recognition, a truck drapes a telephone pole near Kennard, Indiana. One of 148 tornadoes that ravaged 13 states on April 3 and 4, 1974, the storm that wrecked this truck produced winds of more than 200 mph.

A tornado that struck Bossier City, Louisiana, on December 3, 1978, turned a 24-foot steel beam into a javelin, hurling it eight feet into the ground.

During a 1973 twister in Plainview, Texas, a wooden two-by-four broached a brick wall. Though the effect is startling, engineers calculated that it was produced by winds of only 80 mph.

Stripped of its tail and back feathers, a chicken perches on wreckage left by a 1977 tornado in Birmingham, Alabama. A respected consulting firm once suggested that the strength of a tornado could be measured by the number of feathers lost by chickens in its path.

menaced by tornadoes, such considerations are mainly academic. What matters most is the frightful force that tornadoes can generate by both their winds and their updrafts.

Examples are legion. An 1879 tornado in Irving, Kansas, tore an iron bridge from its foundation and twisted it into a useless pile of scrap. After a tornado struck Lubbock, Texas, in 1970, a fertilizer tank 41 feet long and weighing 26,000 pounds was found three quarters of a mile from its original position; investigators could not say for sure that it had been airborne for the entire distance, but its path took it across a four-lane highway and an access road, neither of which showed any damage.

Frequently reported are trees that have been impaled by straws—an oddity explained by the fact that tornadic winds have bent the trees' trunks and opened the pores. One person was killed and more than 60 were injured in 1931 when a tornado roared through Moorhead, Minnesota, dipped down on the *Empire Builder,* an express train traveling at 60 miles per hour, snatched up five of its 70-ton coaches and then dropped them to earth again, one of them 80 feet away. Another twister lofted an 800-pound ice chest for three miles, and still another carried an entire church steeple for 15 miles.

Against such overpowering energies, man's resources seem frail indeed. In the United States, the weather service in 1954 established in Kansas City, Missouri, a Severe Storms Forecast Center, charged among other things with issuing tornado forecasts. A decade later, the weather service set up the National Severe Storms Laboratory in Norman, Oklahoma, which was dedicated to the more basic business of studying the dynamics of tornadoes and other severe storms. Yet despite this massive effort on every level from the theoretical to the practical, including the use of sophisticated technology, the weather service so far has been able to do little more than forecast the general weather conditions that lead to thunderstorms and may—or may not—spawn tornadoes.

The prospects, however, are improving. Since 1971 the National Severe Storms Laboratory has been experimenting with Doppler radar, a device taking its name from the 19th Century Austrian physicist, Christian Doppler, who first noticed that the sound waves from an object approaching the listener increase in their pitch, while those moving away decrease in frequency.

Using this principle, Doppler radar bounces radio signals off the wind-whipped raindrops within storm systems as far as 140 miles away. Receivers at radar stations can detect the higher return frequencies from raindrops blowing toward the antennas and the lower frequencies of those being driven away. High-speed computers analyze the contrasting frequencies and translate them into color patterns on display screens. Increasing degrees of red, for example, would indicate increasing velocities away from the radar, while increasing degrees of green would indicate increasing velocities toward the radar. The presence of a tornado could be detected in the close proximity of two bright contrasting colors—which would signal a swiftly rotating cloud. Operators can thus—in theory at least—spot the distinctive pattern that signals the formation of a tornado within a storm system, and warnings can be issued 20 or even 30 minutes before the deadly funnel touches the ground.

So far, however, the Doppler results have been imperfect. "We missed a few tornadoes," says Donald Burgess, a meteorologist at the Norman laboratory, "and we issued a few false alarms." One problem is that since Doppler radar measures speeds of winds moving toward or away from it, a wind moving at a right angle measures zero velocity. Thus, the radar could fail to give early warning of the tornado potential in a severe squall line moving at a right angle—though it would probably pick up the tightly swirling vortex once it had formed. A second difficulty is that some thunderstorms display a circular wind pattern—and trigger an alert—without ever developing a full-fledged tornado.

T. Theodore Fujita, a pioneer in tornado research at the University of Chicago, demonstrates his tabletop "tornado machine." The ingenious device approximates wind funnels by means of a pan of dry ice to produce a cloud of vapor and an overhead suction fan mounted above spinning cups to impart an upward cyclonic motion.

A small jet carrying meteorologist Theodore Fujita flies over a Mississippi thunderstorm at 45,000 feet on a mission to study the high-altitude characteristics of tornadic storms. Beneath the irregularly formed pileus, or cap cloud *(center and left),* that protrudes above a powerful updraft lies the most likely breeding area for a twister.

The effectiveness of Doppler radar increases dramatically with the number of machines that can be brought to bear on a given storm. Experiments have shown that if one radar fails to yield sufficient information, a second or a third set of electronic eyes viewing the storm from a different angle may provide the answers. The National Weather Service planned to have a broad network of Doppler radar installations operating in the 1990s. Until then, the best hope for coping with tornadoes rests in unlocking the secrets that lie within the twisters themselves. Among those leading the pursuit of knowledge about the nature of tornadoes is a brilliant Japanese-born meteorologist who, to his everlasting disappointment, has never seen a twister from the ground.

Among the diabolic forces unleashed by the atomic bomb that obliterated Hiroshima on August 6, 1945, were several tornadoes, which were caused by heat rising from the burning city into the cooler atmosphere. (Much the same thing had happened in Tokyo during the great earthquake-induced fires of 1923.) Three weeks after the cataclysm a 24-year-old doctoral student named Tetsuya Fujita was on the scene, examining the debris and seeking to draw knowledge from disaster. Ever since, and especially during three decades as a professor of meteorology at the University of Chicago, Fujita—who in 1968 adopted the middle name Theodore—has followed the trail of the twisting winds. "I love tornadoes," he says. "I think I've reached the point of no return. I've almost forgotten why I'm doing this. It has become a passion."

Even during lectures before as many as 200 students, Fujita has been known to announce suddenly: "I'm going to chase tornadoes" and then hurry away. Yet he has never had a satisfactory look at a tornado. (In wry acknowledgement of his frustrations, the license plate on his auto reads "TF-0000.") Fujita is notably unfazed by his failure. "A homicide detective," he says cheerfully, "does not have to see the murder to be a good detective."

During his many years of tornado trailing, Fujita has examined, from airplanes as well as on the ground, more than 2,000 miles of the swaths slashed by approximately 250 tornado systems. Employing another law-and-order analogy, he explains: "Tornadoes are like criminals who cannot get away without leaving their fingerprints." From such clues as the cycloid suction tracks left by tornadoes or the direction in which smashed objects have fallen, Fujita can de-

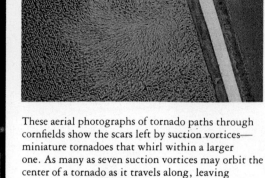

These aerial photographs of tornado paths through cornfields show the scars left by suction vortices—miniature tornadoes that whirl within a larger one. As many as seven suction vortices may orbit the center of a tornado as it travels along, leaving a cycloidal trail of flattened vegetation (*left*); or a small inner whirlwind may spin briefly in one place, leaving a solitary swirl (*above*).

duce an astounding array of facts about tornadic anatomy, motion and velocity.

With his friend Allen Pearson, former chief tornado forecaster for the National Weather Service, Fujita has devised what is now the standard six-point scale for describing the intensity of a tornado on the basis of its wind speed and the damage it causes. A study of almost 26,000 tornadoes since 1916 showed that the great majority fell within the "Light" to "Considerable" damage classifications, while 3,407 were monsters described by Fujita as wreaking "Severe," "Devastating" or "Incredible" damage.

Several years ago, Fujita developed a hypothesis of occasional tornadic "downbursts," which he defines as "strong downdrafts inducing an outward burst of damaging winds on or near the ground." Fujita sees evidence of these downbursts in curious damage patterns in which the debris is spread out in a fan shape, as if struck an oblique blow by a hammer; ordinarily, debris is gathered into spirals by the whirling wind. At first, many of Fujita's colleagues gave little credence to the idea, but after extensive study most of them have come around to his way of thinking. Fujita believes that the downbursts may somehow be responsible for the behavior of rare tornadoes that, contrary to all known laws of nature, rotate clockwise rather than counterclockwise in the Northern Hemisphere.

After working more than a year with a computer programed with the path lengths of 26,000 twisters, Fujita found that American tornadoes have distinct characteristics according to whether they occur west or east of a dividing zone that runs north by northeast from eastern Texas to Michigan's Upper Peninsula. Western tornadoes reach their peak in April and May, while eastern tornadoes are most frequent in March and April. Wind speeds are generally comparable, but the east experiences more superoutbreaks in which many tornadoes ravage the land simultaneously.

Fujita knows a lot about such epidemic tornadoes: He headed a team that followed the tracks of the greatest outbreak known to meteorological history.

During 16 hours and 10 minutes on April 3 and 4, 1974, no fewer than 148 tornadoes rampaged through 13 states, from Alabama and Georgia north to Michigan, and one Canadian province, killing 315 persons, injuring 5,484 others and causing property damage of more than half a billion dollars. Altogether the tornadoes slashed paths totaling 2,598 miles; the mean length of the tracks was 18.7 miles as compared with 4.7 miles for all U.S. tornadoes in 1973 and only 3.3 miles in 1972. Six of the outbreak's tornadoes achieved

F-5 intensity, while only one had arrived at that peak in 1973 and none in 1972. Finally, six cities and towns were stricken, not by one but by two separate tornadoes.

At around 7 a.m. on Wednesday, April 3, a cold front, moving at an average speed of 35 miles per hour beneath high-altitude jet winds, was pushing eastward from the Rockies across Texas. Awaiting it in the Gulf states and Tennessee was an unstable mass of low-lying tropical air. At 8:42 a.m. satellite photographs showed a line of convective activity forming from Lafayette, Louisiana, northeastward to Clarksville, Tennessee, then curving back to near Paducah, Kentucky. By early afternoon, both satellite and radar images defined three ominous squall lines developing: one from Lake Michigan southward through Illinois and into Missouri, a second from southwestern Indiana into western Kentucky and Tennessee, and the third from eastern Tennessee south into northwestern Georgia and southwest through east-central Alabama. Satellite imagery depicted storm-cloud tops reaching as high as 60,000 feet, well above the tropopause—a sure sign of severe activity.

At 1:10 p.m., a small tornado touched down near Morris, Illinois, without doing damage. Around 2 o'clock twisters appeared in Bradley County, Tennessee, and Gilmer County, Georgia; within 10 minutes tornadoes struck McLean and Logan Counties in Illinois; at 2:20 murderous whirlwinds set down in Indiana's Perry and Lawrence Counties, and others were soon reported in Ohio, Kentucky and Alabama. At 7 p.m. the frenzy came to a crescendo as 15 tornadoes ripped simultaneously across the afflicted region. The nightmare continued until 9 a.m. on April 4, when the last tornado hit North Carolina.

Within 24 hours, Fujita was inspecting the blighted area as director of a five-man university team operating in conjunction with investigators sent in by the National Oceanic and Atmospheric Administration. Mapping the paths and calculating the strengths of all 148 tornadoes, Fujita and his colleagues sought a meteorological profile of the unprecedented outbreak. To their surprise they found that many of the tornadoes had hugged the ground despite adverse topography. In Georgia, for example, one tornado had crossed a 3,000-foot

The tornado intensity scale below, devised by meteorologist T. Theodore Fujita in 1971, classifies tornadoes according to the damage they cause. Each F rating correlates with a range of wind speeds; the speeds reflect a combination of rotational and forward velocity. As seen in the photos, tornadoes classified as F-1 and F-2 affect mainly windows and roofs; F-3 winds can collapse outer walls. Winds rated F-4 can reduce an entire house to rubble; F-5 winds obliterate the structure and carry away much of the debris.

FUJITA TORNADO INTENSITY SCALE

Rating	MPH	Expected Damage
F-0	40-72	LIGHT DAMAGE
F-1	73-112	MODERATE DAMAGE
F-2	113-157	CONSIDERABLE DAMAGE
F-3	158-206	SEVERE DAMAGE
F-4	207-260	DEVASTATING DAMAGE
F-5	261-318	INCREDIBLE DAMAGE

F-1

F-2

F-3

F-4

F-5

ridge, descended to the bottom of a 1,000-foot canyon and then climbed to the top of a 3,300-foot ridge on the opposite side of the canyon. The track astonished Fujita because tornadoes in the confines of a canyon usually die for lack of vast masses of air. This tornado had to be of great intensity—and the damage patterns confirmed that it was in the F-4 category, with winds as high as 260 miles per hour.

Although knowledge of such tornadic behavior would be of great help to meteorologists, the full impact of the events of April 3 and 4, 1974, could only be understood in terms of terror and human suffering. In northwestern Alabama, 19 persons were killed, most of them in the little town of Guin, where a state trooper later reported: "Guin just isn't there." At Jasper, 40 miles away, the city hall was destroyed, and a radio announcer told his listeners: "We can't talk to the police department—it just blew away." The town of Tanner was hit by two tornadoes, one at 7 p.m. and the other a half hour later. The first twister smashed down a brick house and killed all six of its occupants, carrying them 250 feet and dumping them into a pine forest.

In Indiana, 17-year-old Karen Scott was with five friends in a Volkswagen bus crossing a bridge over an arm of Lake Freeman; a tornado blasted the vehicle into the water 50 feet away. She managed to escape from the bus and swim to safety, but her companions were killed. In Brandenburg, Kentucky, 29 persons died, most of them children playing outside after school; days later, relatives were still trying to identify some of the mangled bodies. In Sugar Valley, Georgia, a tornado picked up nine-year-old Randall Goble and carried him 200 yards before flinging him back to the ground. Taken to a hospital, he cried

Scattered like jackstraws, the splintered remains of a Louisville, Kentucky, neighborhood bear testimony to the fantastic power of a tornado that swept through the city on April 3, 1974. One of scores of twisters that roared across the central United States on that fateful day, this particular tornado carried 250-mph winds and destroyed 900 homes in 20 minutes.

The slashes on this map chart the paths of more than 140 tornadoes that whirled across 13 states and Canada during a 16-hour superoutbreak on April 3 and 4, 1974. The strikingly parallel paths, adding up to 2,598 miles of devastation, illustrate the propensity of North American tornadoes to travel, with the thunderstorms that spawn them, in a northeasterly direction.

to a nurse: "Tell me it was a bad dream. Where's my mommy and daddy?" His mother, his father and his two sisters were later found dead in one room of their wrecked home.

The most sorely smitten city in the region was Xenia, Ohio (population 27,000), where 34 persons perished and almost 3,000 homes and other buildings were destroyed or damaged. Yet Xenia was, in a way, fortunate: Because the tornado that tore a 3,000-foot-wide path through its heart came after school hours, most of the students were gone from the five schools that were demolished. At Xenia High School, however, Ruth Venuti, 18, was waiting for a friend to drive her home when, at 4:25, she saw a large black cloud about two and a half miles away. As she watched through a doorway, the cloud began changing into a revolving horizontal configuration. "I realized it was a tornado," she later recalled, "when I saw the air currents begin to swirl."

Remembering that 15 members of the school's drama club were rehearsing in the auditorium at the other end of the building, Ruth Venuti ran to alert them. At first the club's director, English teacher David Heath, thought she was joking. "I came very close to telling everyone to forget it and to go through a dance number they were rehearsing again," Heath said later. "Instead I jumped off the stage and told everyone to follow me so we could get a view of the tornado. I imagined a funnel cloud in the sky that we could look at and then return to rehearsing."

Rather than witnessing some sort of exciting spectacle, the astonished group saw a viciously twisting column less than 200 yards away. "Then," said Heath, "cars parked in front of the school began to bounce around. It was beyond belief. Someone said we'd better take cover so we all ran toward the center hall of the school. The lights went out just before we turned the corner and crouched against the walls on both sides of the corridor."

Instants later the tornado struck with "a noise like the clattering of a thousand sets of Venetian blinds, along with tremendous crashing and grating sounds. When I opened my eyes a couple of times I saw large pieces of dirt and wood flying horizontally down the corridor." Then, for a moment, the wind subsided as the tornado's eye passed over the building. One boy started to stand but Heath yelled at him to get down. "Then the wind hit again with seemingly greater force," Heath said. "We were all hit with dirt, broken glass, mud, wood, Heaven knows what else. I was still picking glass out of my scalp two days later. Finally it stopped, and there was total silence."

No one was killed or even seriously injured. But the entire top floor of the high school had been swept away. Part of the roof had collapsed into the auditorium vacated by the drama club. And on the stage where they had been rehearsing lay a school bus, upside down.

From beginning to end, the ordeal of the students at Xenia High School had lasted but four minutes. Ω

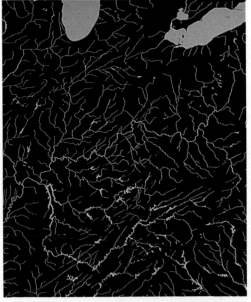

AN ANATOMY OF THUNDERSTORMS AND TORNADOES

When several cumulus clouds combine, they insulate a central updraft of moist, warm air, which races upward at speeds as high as 30 mph. The edges of the updraft mix surrounding air into the cumulonimbus and sculpt its crisp, billowy shape.

At roughly 45,000 feet, rising air inside a cumulonimbus collides with the tropopause, a border where air temperature starts to become warmer with increasing height. The central updraft penetrates the tropopause for a few thousand feet, but the warmer surrounding air quickly halts convection and flattens the thunderhead's top into an anvil-shaped cloud of ice crystals (dashes). In the storm's lower reaches, condensing snow (stars) and rain (dots) gradually outweigh the updrafts and drag air down as they begin to fall.

Although thunderstorms are best known for jagged bolts of lightning and the roll of celestial kettledrums, their real role is to act as a heat pump for the planet. Like hurricanes, thunderstorms transfer heat from the earth's surface to the atmosphere, where it can be radiated back into space. Without this heat exchange one third of the solar energy absorbed by the earth would be trapped at the surface, raising temperatures worldwide by nearly 20° F.

A thunderstorm's remarkable heat capacity is due largely to the unusual thermal properties of water. When a gallon of water evaporates on the surface, it cools the earth

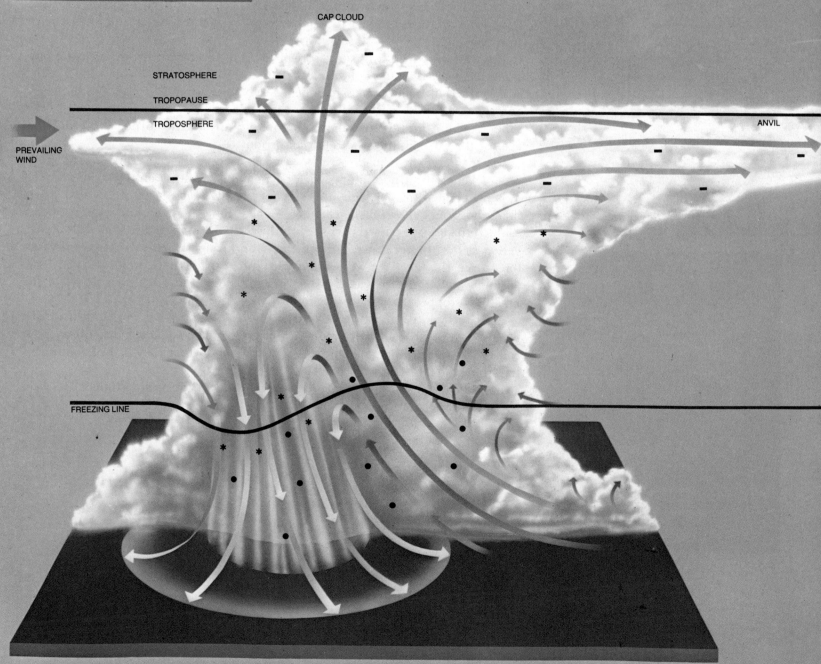

by carrying into the atmosphere two million calories of energy as latent heat. In a thunderstorm this vapor condenses into towering clouds, releasing the latent heat five or more miles up in the atmosphere. All rainstorms pump heat into the atmosphere in this fashion, but thunderstorms are particularly efficient because of their tremendous height.

A thunderstorm begins when low-lying parcels of moist, warm air begin to rise by convection: As the parcels absorb heat they expand and become less dense, then float upward through cooler, heavier air just as air bubbles float up through water. The ascent often is started by uneven heating from the earth's surface; the air above a smokestack or a sunny forest, for example, rises by convection. Or the parcels may be lifted mechanically, usually by a wind that blows low-lying air over a mountain range.

But like all expanding gases the rising parcels cool as their pressure decreases, just as a pressurized gas cools when it rushes out of a spray can. This effect is only partly counterbalanced above the condensation line, as latent heat in water vapor is released by the formation of cumulus clouds.

The future of these clouds depends on the atmosphere's temperature profile. In winter the air temperature at higher altitudes usually drops more slowly than the temperature of the rising parcels, producing what meteorologists consider a stable atmosphere. The parcels grow colder than the surrounding air and convection ceases.

But in summer, heat builds up near the earth's surface while high-altitude air remains cold, so the temperature gradient steepens dramatically. When the temperature drops more than about 4° F. per 1,000 feet of altitude, cumulus clouds soar unhindered and eventually aggregate into a single towering cumulonimbus—the majestic thunderhead.

As the storm breaks, the cold downdraft from the precipitation quickly quells the updraft, then hits the ground and fans outward into a powerful gust front that sweeps ahead of the rain. Atop the dissipating storm, high-altitude winds stretch the ice-laden anvil for as much as 500 miles.

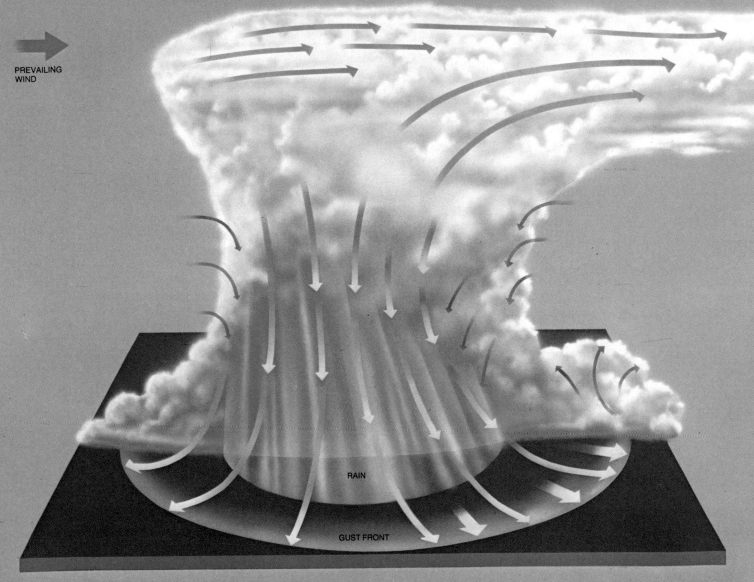

PREVAILING
WIND

RAIN

GUST FRONT

DISSIPATING STORM

DISSIPATING STORM

MATURE STO

MATURE STORM

SUPERCELL STORM

DEVELOPING STORMS

DEVELOPING STORMS

COLD F

WARM, MOIST AIR

Squall Lines and Supercells

In meteorological terms, isolated summer thundershowers are locally impressive but not especially dangerous. Yet a squall line hundreds of miles long and containing perhaps 50 thunderheads is a force to be reckoned with. Such a phalanx of storms, one reinforcing the other, can generate winds of more than 100 miles per hour.

Squall lines may form when several isolated storms combine, but they usually arise from large-scale collisions between cold air and a tongue of warm air. Frequently a dense cold front underrides the warm air, pushing it upward; the warm air then soars through colder regions by convection alone. In other cases convection is initiated by prefrontal waves, poorly understood disturbances that lift moist air as much as 150 miles ahead of the front.

Once a squall line starts, several factors frequently combine to redouble its strength. If a strong cumulus cloud finally breaches a low-level inversion—a layer where air temperature increases with al-

titude, blocking weak convection—the moist air trapped beneath the inversion surges through the resulting hole to build a few severe storms. Dry air above the inversion chills each cloud's edges by evaporation, widening the temperature gap between the warm central updraft and cold surrounding air, and thus accelerating the updraft. Moreover, strong high-altitude winds above the squall line can act as a sort of exhaust fan for updrafts, literally vacuuming up lower-level air.

Most squall line storms die within an hour or so, although the squall line itself may continue for many hours. But squall lines also contain rare supercells—long-lived, rotating storms of exceptional violence (opposite). The exact sources of rotation remain an enigma, but they include the Coriolis effect of the earth's rotation and vorticity, the rotation generated by the varying speed and curvature of the wind. Once started, the supercell's rotation sets the stage for a tornado.

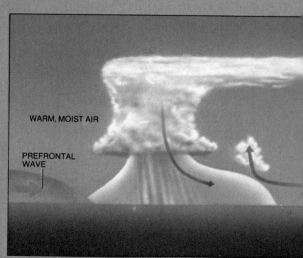

WARM, MOIST AIR

PREFRONTAL WAVE

A squall line commonly begins when an advancing cold front or a prefrontal wave wedges beneath a warm, moist layer to start the convective cycle (inset). The resulting line of thunderstorms (top), which sweeps forward at perhaps 40 mph, perpetuates itself automatically: As each thunderstorm breaks and dissipates, its cold gust front underrides more warm air and gives birth to another storm. Tornado-bearing supercells often are located at the southern end of the squall line, which thrives on the southerly tongue of warm air and siphons it away from the other storms.

PREFRONTAL WAVE

GUST FRONT

In a supercell thunderstorm *(below)*, the violent updrafts converge in a sharply defined wall cloud that hovers only 1,500 feet above the ground, then spirals up at perhaps 60 mph. It eventually shoots several miles above the tropopause, creating a huge cap cloud. Because raindrops have no time to grow in such a swift updraft, rain is concentrated in a dark hook *(right)* around the updraft. Tornadoes usually form from the updraft at the hook's tip *(red dot)*, where the wind speed and spin are greatest.

RAIN HOOK

CENTRAL UPDRAFT

● TORNADO

CAP CLOUD

TROPOPAUSE

SPIRAL UPDRAFT

WALL CLOUD

GUST FRONT

The Ultimate Storm

The twister is a prodigy of nature. A screaming roar assaults the ears, missiles weighing more than a ton hurtle through the air, scythelike winds cut down the sturdiest of structures. All this fearsome power is concentrated in a narrow swath between 10 and 400 yards wide—and therein lies the key to the tornado's strength.

Any rotating object, such as a ball on a string, speeds up when pulled toward its axis of rotation, thus conserving its angular momentum. Rotating winds behave similarly when a strong low-pressure center created by a supercell thunderstorm sucks them inward: A five-mile-an-hour zephyr circling four miles from the center, for example, contains enough energy to fuel a 160-mile-an-hour tornado 400 yards wide.

Although some rare twisters wreak havoc for hours, the life span of most is mercifully brief—less than 15 minutes on the average. A typical tornado descends from a severe thunderstorm as a crisp white funnel cloud. When it touches ground the twister quickly turns gray with dust and soon develops ragged edges. In the end a tornado in effect becomes clogged with air. Although it still can generate swirling winds, a weakening tornado no longer can suck up the air in its path and gradually lags behind its parent thunderhead. The funnel stretches into a sinuous, ropy shape and eventually dissipates altogether.

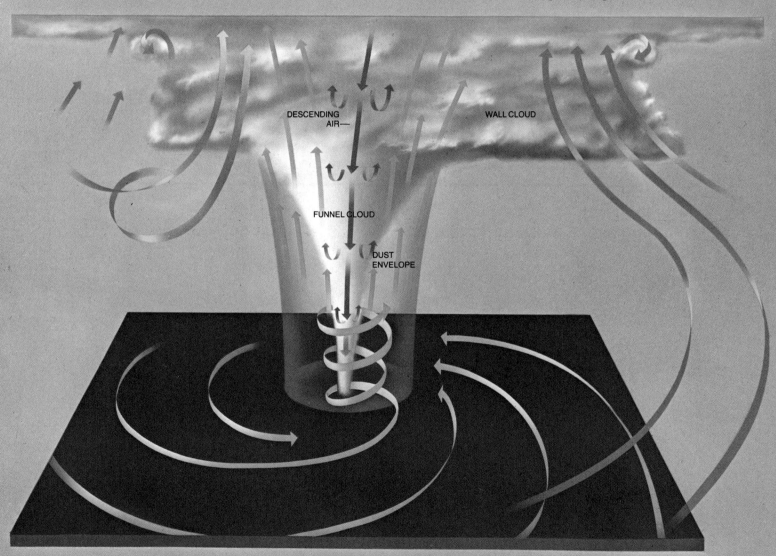

In many respects a tornado resembles a miniature hurricane: Within the dust envelope, the strongest updrafts surround a calm central eye of low pressure, where air gently descends from above. Because a tornado's lowest pressure is located just above the ground (*inset*), air sucked into the vortex at first gains speed as it spirals around the eye, then gradually slows inside the overhanging cumulonimbus. This pressure configuration also accounts for a tornado's shape: The initial thin, white cloud is caused by condensation along a funnel-shaped low-pressure line.

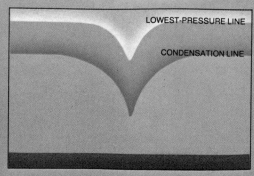

Within a large tornado, turbulent eddies often generate an ongoing series of miniature twisters called suction vortices, which are the most violent whirlwinds on earth. Each vortex usually circles the tornado's center for less than one revolution, sometimes hidden in the dust cloud, frequently as a separate funnel 10 to 100 feet wide. But because vortices combine three wind components— their own rotation, rotation around the tornado and the tornado's forward movement—they generate winds up to 100 miles per hour stronger than those elsewhere in the tornado. The haphazard birth of these tiny, sharply defined twisters, each with a life span of mere minutes, accounts for the freakish damage from many tornadoes: A vortex can slash through a house like a knife, obliterating one half and sparing the other, then disappear and leave the rest of the neighborhood untouched.

SUCTION VORTEX

SUCTION VORTEX

SUCTION VORTEX

TORNADO PATH

Chapter 6

ATTEMPTING TO TAME THE WEATHER

In the last 19 months man has learned to control the weather." So declared *Fortune,* a publication by no means given to reckless statements, in February 1948. *Fortune* went on to quote Nobel Prize-winning chemist Irving Langmuir regarding some specific benefits that appeared to be within the grasp of science: "I think there is a reasonable probability that in one or two years man will be able to abolish most damage effects from hurricanes."

Those were heady days, thanks largely to experiments in which Langmuir himself played a leading part, and the optimists had reason to believe they were right. Yet more than 30 years later, mankind's dream of moderating the destructive forces of storm remained far from reality. Moreover, in the face of complex legal, economic and environmental problems, the question of whether science could alter storms had been shadowed by doubts as to whether it should.

Until that dilemma could be resolved, the official attitude of the United States—world leader in pursuit of the vision—was best described in a report by a 1978 advisory board to the Secretary of Commerce: "The prime requirement of a national weather modification policy is to learn more about the atmosphere itself." Put to its most practical purpose, this aim results in improved forecasting—to the end that even without attempting to dilute the concentrated fury of storms, meteorologists can at least provide sufficient warning for prospective victims to remove themselves from harm's way.

The effort has been successful to a degree that would have confounded the ancient Greeks and might have moved Ferdinand of Tuscany, that remarkable 17th Century patron of weather science, to lift a goblet in a toast of appreciation. Indeed, backed by an ever-increasing understanding of the nature of storms, and by a dazzling array of meteorological, data-analyzing and communications instrumentation and equipment, weather forecasting has evolved into one of the greatest and most cooperative global enterprises ever undertaken by mankind.

Still, the hope that scientists will one day exercise significant control over the behavior of storms remains a tantalizing possibility. In its modern incarnation weather modification was conceived in a General Electric Company laboratory in Schenectady, New York, and was, as Langmuir later described it, a classic example of "scientific serendipity"—the ability to turn the unexpected to advantage.

As a chemist at the Schenectady research facility, Langmuir had earned a Nobel Prize for his work in explaining the astounding potency of such tiny things as molecules and electrons, and the extraordinary strength of thin films floating on water. During World War II, at the government's behest, Langmuir and fellow G.E. chemist Vincent Schaefer had undertaken a study of the cloud-borne water

A satellite image of cloud patterns taken from 500 miles above the earth helps a forecaster at the Joint Typhoon Warning Center in Guam determine the strength and track of a Pacific storm. Under the powerful illuminated magnifier, areas as small as a half mile across are clearly visible.

149

droplets that freeze and form ice and rime on the wings of airplanes. The project took them to New Hampshire's 6,288-foot-high Mount Washington, where they spent several weeks during the last two winters of the War.

In the moisture of the clouds swirling about the mountaintop, Langmuir and Schaefer found a mystery. Though the temperature in the clouds frequently dropped far below freezing, it often happened that only a few ice crystals formed amid the billions of supercooled droplets in a cloud. Yet sometimes an unknown natural mechanism would suddenly turn a cloud into a blizzard of ice or snow. The question confounding the two chemists was, of course, what triggered the transformation—and after the War, they returned to Schenectady to find out.

Just as Langmuir was a brilliant theoretician, Schaefer was a superb experimentalist. A onetime machinist who had never finished high school, he took his tinkering talents to the laboratory, where he taught himself chemistry. Now, to probe into the secrets of supercooled water, he used an ordinary $240 General Electric home freezer, lining it with black velvet and using a strong light for better visibility—and expelling his own breath into it to produce a cloud.

The idea was to cause snow by introducing bits of foreign matter into the vapor of Schaefer's breath. Behind that notion lay a principle formulated in the 1930s in Europe, where several meteorologists had theorized that a cloud might be considered as an aerosol—a suspension in air of fine solid or liquid particles. Virtually weightless, the particles could fall only if they grew; growth was stimulated when ice crystals appeared within formations of vapor and supercooled water droplets. The water molecules diffused onto the ice crystals, which became large and heavy enough to start falling as snowflakes or, if they melted on the way to the ground, as rain.

But what caused the ice crystals to form in the first place? The Europeans surmised that the process required the presence in the atmosphere of unknown but specific types of particles—which they called sublimation, or condensation, nuclei. And it was in quest of these particles that Schaefer went to work with his freezer. In more than 100 experiments, he tried fine grains of such substances as volcanic dust, graphite, carbon, sugar, salt, talc and soap powder. Nothing happened, even when the freezer reached its mechanical lower limit of $-9°$ F.

Then, while alone in the lab on a torrid July day in 1946, Schaefer had trouble getting his freezer as cold as he wanted it. To lower the temperature, he put in a piece of dry ice—carbon dioxide frozen solid at $-109.3°$ F. —and almost instantly saw millions of ice motes form, grow into small flakes and flurry to the freezer's velvet floor in a miniature snowstorm.

It was obvious that the snow had been induced by the extreme cold created by the dry ice within the freezer—and Schaefer's search for the elusive condensation nuclei was preempted. The Schenectady scientists found that $-40°$ F. was the critical temperature at which supercooled water began turning into ice crystals. The irresistible next step was to use dry ice to create a snowstorm in nature.

On November 13, 1946, Schaefer rented a small plane and, at an altitude of 14,000 feet 30 miles east of Schenectady, found a supercooled stratus cloud that suited his purpose. Leaning out of the plane's window, he sowed six pounds of dry-ice pellets along a four-mile stretch. Within moments, the tranquil cloud was in turmoil—and in less than five minutes a curtain of snow was falling to earth. Though it fell only 2,000 feet before melting and evaporating, Schaefer had accomplished his goal. Proclaimed Langmuir: "This is history!"

Two subsequent tests showed similar results and another was scheduled for the next month. On December 19, the weather forecast for the following day was "fair and warmer." But when Schaefer seeded a cloud with dry ice on December 20, the winter's heaviest snowfall began. Eight inches piled up in northern New York and Vermont. Traffic was snarled, scores of auto accidents were reported and shoppers stayed home—with a consequent loss of business to merchants.

General Electric's legal department came awake with a start: Could the com-

A French newspaper published in 1901 illustrated a presumptuous early attempt at weather modification with antihail cannon, sheet-metal funnels 10 feet tall loaded with three ounces of gunpowder. The hope was that the blast would shatter the hail and produce a "fine and gentle shower" that would nourish, rather than flatten, valuable crops. But the only effect was a loud bang.

pany be held legally responsible for damages caused by the snowstorm its scientists had apparently created? Langmuir and Schaefer issued a disclaimer: "We do not believe that this snowstorm was caused by our seeding experiments." But G.E. was taking no more chances—as far as the corporation was concerned, Schaefer was grounded.

Work in the Schenectady laboratory, however, was allowed to continue, and the abandoned search for condensation nuclei was now resumed. Among those analyzing the problem was Bernard Vonnegut, a 32-year-old chemist who had been studying the properties of supercooled tin. Like Schaefer before him, Vonnegut embarked on a random program, trying one thing after another without any particular pattern. Then, while driving home from work one day, he was struck by an idea: Why not try to trick nature by introducing as sublimation nuclei the particles of a substance whose crystal structure closely resembled that of ice? Referring to his *Handbook of Chemistry and Physics,* which lists more than 1,300 compounds, Vonnegut quickly struck upon silver iodide, whose hexagonal crystalline structure almost matched that of ice crystals.

Vonnegut's first laboratory test was a flop; his commercially purchased silver iodide was impure. But when he tried again with pure silver iodide the results were spectacular. The tiniest amount was enough to produce snow, and Langmuir later calculated that only 200 pounds of the stuff would suffice to seed the world's entire atmosphere.

At this point General Electric bowed out of the field experiments, and sponsorship was jointly taken over in early 1947 by the U.S. Army Signal Corps and the Office of Naval Research. With Langmuir and Schaefer on loan as advisers, the military establishments launched Project Cirrus, the first large-scale scientific study of cloud physics and weather modification. Among its purposes was a venture hitherto deemed hopelessly beyond man's reach. In its most ambitious aspect, Project Cirrus aimed at modifying one of the mightiest and most violent of all weather phenomena—the hurricane.

Project Cirrus was the first attempt to make practical use of the lessons learned at G.E.'s Schenectady laboratory. The scientists wanted to find out whether they could control the timing and area of precipitation and induce changes in cloud content and formation. For months they seeded clouds and gathered data all over the United States. By late 1947 the scientists were ready to attempt the seeding of a hurricane in the hope that its winds could be diminished.

The first attempt to defuse a hurricane took place on October 13, 1947—and for the men who were audacious enough to believe they could tame the monster storms, it was a setback, one from which the endeavor would not soon recover.

Traveling from west to east, the second worst hurricane of the year had already battered Miami and, its force beginning to dwindle, was 350 miles out at sea when a Project Cirrus B-17 bomber made three seeding passes, dropping a total of 180 pounds of dry ice. Project Cirrus officials later reported that there had been "pronounced modification of the cloud deck seeded," but could produce no evidence that the effort had caused the storm's winds to abate.

Far from it. By the next day the hurricane again had gathered strength and, having virtually reversed its eastward course, slammed into Savannah, Georgia, causing widespread damage and killing one person. A weather bureau forecaster in Miami somewhat impetuously pronounced it "entirely possible" that the seeding had "contributed to the unusual behavior of the storm." Lawsuits were threatened and were dropped only in the face of evidence that the hurricane had already begun to turn when the seeding occurred and that a 1906 storm had followed almost exactly the same course.

Then and since, weather modifiers have insisted that seeding can neither divert a hurricane from its track nor significantly increase the gross volume of its precipitation. But the 1947 scare was nonetheless sufficient to force a halt to operations—and not for 11 years was another hurricane seeding test made.

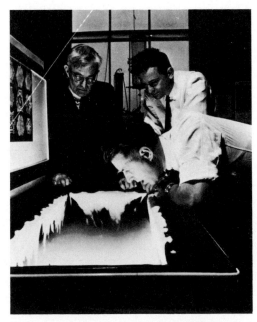

Breathing into a freezer to create a miniature cloud of supercooled water droplets, Vincent J. Schaefer, a pioneer in weather modification research, prepares for a cloud seeding experiment in 1946. Moments later he tossed tiny pieces of dry ice into the freezer; the temperature was thus lowered and the droplets were immediately transformed into ice crystals. Such forced precipitation is the principle behind efforts to modify storm behavior through cloud seeding.

In 1956, the U.S. Weather Bureau established a National Hurricane Research Project, and three years later planes, now loaded with silver iodide instead of dry ice, were sent out four times to seed Hurricane Daisy. The equipment broke down during three attempts, so that despite improved instruments, calculations of reduced wind speeds were far from conclusive. In 1961 the seeding of Hurricane Esther again brought questionable results.

Despite the disappointments, the believers remained believers, and in 1962, with Project Cirrus dead for a decade, the U.S. Weather Bureau and the U.S. Navy joined hands in Project Stormfury—the most concentrated effort ever undertaken to bring hurricane forces to leash.

The theory behind the effort was a marvel of ingenuity. It held that seeding the clouds in a hurricane eye wall with silver iodide would, by accelerating the transformation of liquid water into ice, release the latent heat of fusion and increase the temperature at the outer edges of the eye wall. When this occurred, the typically sharp drop in atmospheric pressure across the eye wall would be vastly reduced, since the temperature differential had decreased. Relieved of the pressure forces that kept it in its tight spiral, the eye wall would open and—just as extending the arms can slow the spin of a skater—the speed of the hurricane's winds would be checked, with consequences beneficial to mankind.

The next year, after Hurricane Beulah was seeded, airborne radar indicated that the storm's eye wall had indeed weakened and that wind speeds had decreased by 10 to 15 per cent. This, though encouraging, was hardly proof of success; the same things could have happened naturally, without any help from silver iodide. Then, in the late summer of 1965, came Stormfury's best opportunity—which, like the 1947 test, was to arouse a tempest of controversy.

Toward the end of August 1965, meteorologists following the progress of Hurricane Betsy decided that it was a likely seeding target. The storm was small

A long, narrow depression in a deck of supercooled clouds mirrors the flight path of the aircraft that seeded the area with crushed dry ice as part of a 1947 attempt at weather modification. Though the United States government program produced equivocal results, this particular experiment succeeded: The supercooled cloud droplets formed ice crystals that fell as a snow shower.

This diagram charts the wind speeds at various distances from the center of Hurricane Debbie before and after five seedings with silver iodide on August 18, 1969. Debbie's eye increased in diameter as a result of the seedings—and this widening in turn temporarily slowed the winds spinning around the eye by as much as 30 per cent.

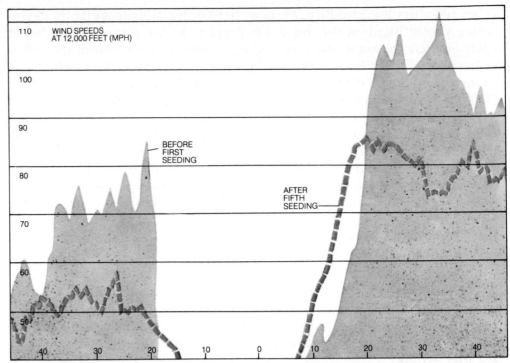

WIND SPEEDS
AT 12,000 FEET (MPH)

110
100
90
80
70
60
50

BEFORE
FIRST
SEEDING

AFTER
FIFTH
SEEDING

40   30   20   10   0   10   20   30   40

DISTANCE IN MILES FROM HURRICANE CENTER

and compact, with a clearly defined wall around its eye. The scientists made plans to send out their planes. They were, however, working under restrictions: Having learned a lesson from the 1947 disaster, Stormfury's project directors decreed that no attempt could be made to seed any storm that had more than a 10 per cent chance of coming within 60 miles of populated land within 24 hours.

Even as the scientists watched, their hopes for Betsy sank: Swerving from northwest to west, the storm seemed to be taking a dead aim on the Bahamas. On September 1, Stormfury officials decided that they could not risk seeding and canceled the effort. In an oversight the project's directors would have reason to rue, someone forgot to notify all of the press, and a few newspapers reported that the cloud seeding was actually under way.

In the event, Betsy roared northwestward just east of the Bahamas, missing them by only 150 miles, and ran head-on into a huge high-pressure area that stretched across the northeastern United States and far out into the Atlantic. Deflected by this high-pressure zone, Betsy turned and smashed ashore along the south Florida coast. The repercussions this time stirred the ire of Congress. It took two months for Stormfury officials to convince Congress that cloud seeding was blameless for Betsy's abrupt change of course.

Stormfury was finally allowed to continue, and the project's equipment was gradually improved. The crude method of dumping dry ice or silver iodide crystals gave way to rocket canisters, then to wing-mounted guns that fired silver iodide into the clouds. Airborne wind-measuring instruments were refined. During the same period, the scientific hypothesis on which the seeding was based became much more sophisticated. The modified theory took into account the presence of cumulus towers embedded in the storm system outside the hurricane eye wall. Seeding the areas in which such towers are known to exist, according to the new thinking, could, by the liberation of latent energy, create new convectional conduits—in effect, new hurricane eye walls—and cause the original eye wall to collapse for lack of sustaining energy. Because an eye wall created by seeding would presumably be broader than the old one, the winds around the eye would spiral less tightly and would therefore be of reduced velocity.

In 1969 came the best chance yet to put the hypothesis to test—Hurricane Debbie, a splendid storm from the would-be seeders' point of view. A well-formed tropical cyclone, Debbie threatened no land masses, yet its course took it within 700 miles of Puerto Rico, the outer limit of operating range for the cloud-seeding aircraft based on the island. On August 18, five planes carrying silver iodide canisters and eight planes packed with monitoring equipment took off at regular intervals from Puerto Rico and headed for a rendezvous with Debbie.

One after another, the seeding planes flew into Debbie's towering clouds at 33,000 feet, dropping hundreds of canisters that were set to explode and spread silver iodide smoke through the clouds just outside the storm's eye wall. Meanwhile, some of the observers circled the storm at altitudes of 37,000 and 1,000 feet, while others made runs at 12,000 feet through the heart of the hurricane. What they found was impressive: After the fifth seeding of the day, Debbie's winds had gone from 112 miles per hour to 78, a decrease of 30 per cent.

The next day, the observation planes went out alone to study Debbie. Without seeding, the hurricane's winds had picked up to 113 miles per hour. On the third day, August 20, both seeding and monitoring planes went out again. By the end of the day, Debbie's winds had diminished to 96 miles per hour, a 16 per cent decrease.

Ninety-six miles per hour—even 78 miles per hour—is still above official hurricane wind speed. But a decrease of 20 to 30 per cent is significant. Since the impact of wind on structures is proportional to the square of its speed, the potential destructiveness of Debbie's blasts had been reduced by up to 50 per cent after seeding.

But Stormfury's major success with Hurricane Debbie proved impossible to duplicate in the ensuing years. Atlantic hurricanes meeting the stringent safety rules for seeding proved frustrating in their infrequency. Because there are more typhoons than hurricanes, Stormfury planned to move its area of concentration to the Pacific, with its major base of operations on the island of Guam. Yet here, diplomatic considerations impeded the seeders: The government of the People's Republic of China, still fearful that seeding might change the course of typhoons, let it be known that it would not appreciate a diversion that afflicted its shores; the Japanese, even more adamant, noted that they receive more than half of their precious rainfall from typhoons and declared themselves more than willing to put up with any inconveniences the great storms might cause.

Meanwhile, efforts to moderate the effects of other types of storms met with similar setbacks.

The vast vistas of the Soviet Union have throughout history been peculiarly susceptible to the bombardments of hailstones. Yet in the early 1960s, Soviet scientists reported remarkable success in the suppression of hail's devastating effect on agriculture. By 1972, according to official reports, some two and a half million acres of crops were under government protection against hail, and in the Caucasus granary the program had been 70 to 95 per cent effective.

Western scientists had long since become at least somewhat skeptical of Soviet claims, yet this one seemed to make sense. The basic—and enticingly simple—idea was that heavy cloud seeding would create astronomical numbers of small hailstones that would either melt during their descent or arrive as harmless tiny pellets, rather than pounding the earth with large icy conglomerates.

In 1972 the U.S. National Center for Atmospheric Research began a hail research experiment to test the Soviet approach, and Guy G. Goyer, the program's first director, was very optimistic: "Of all the severe storms plaguing humanity, the hailstorm appears to be the most manageable." The United States tried one seeding effort after another in northeastern Colorado, a region so besieged by hailstorms it is known as Hail Alley. But nothing seemed to work, and by 1977 a leading researcher in a National Science Foundation study was moved to admit: "At present there is no established hail suppression technology."

In much the same manner, hopes for mitigating the effects of lightning were balked. During the 1960s the U.S. Forest Service, in a project given the vivid

When the first weather satellite hurtled into space on April 1, 1960, its fuzzy television pictures heralded a new era in meteorology. For the first time forecasters could actually see huge weather patterns that previously had been visible only in arcane isobars on the twice-daily weather map.

But even this new Television and Infrared Observation Satellite (TIROS) did not give a truly global view of the weather. Its orbit traversed only narrow bands on the spinning planet and failed to cover the polar regions that determine much of the earth's weather.

Today more powerful rockets allow forecasters to solve these problems with two different types of spacecraft. Four geostationary satellites—two of them American GOES, the space-age acronym for Geostationary Operational Environmental Satellite—circle 22,300 miles above the Equator, an altitude that matches a satellite's orbital period to the earth's rotation. From there each GOES can photograph the unfolding weather within a circle 7,000 miles wide in 18 minutes. Or it can be instructed by radio to scan a smaller sector in less than 10 minutes—a capability that is particularly useful in tracking tropical cyclones.

To observe polar fronts, which often are beyond the horizon of the equatorial GOES series, forecasters use two polar-orbiting TIROS-N craft, third-generation versions of the durable 1960 TIROS. Each TIROS-N orbits about 14 times a day, transmitting 1,000 pictures to three ground stations. Computers then put together polar photo mosaics like the one on page 83.

Although both GOES and TIROS-N have a full battery of instruments, the mainstay is a radiometer—a sophisticated electronic camera that takes photographs in visible wavelengths and, equally valuable to meteorologists, takes infrared pictures of the earth's heat. The GOES radiometers and special units on TIROS-N also can make atmospheric soundings, which measure temperature and moisture at different altitudes. These data yield a host of additional insights for severe-storm forecasters: the sea-surface temperature ahead of a tropical cyclone, for example, or the intensity of potentially tornadic thunderstorms.

Encased in a white ceramic fairing, the 875-pound GOES-East soars skyward atop a three-stage Delta rocket and its ring of solid-fuel boosters on May 22, 1981. After the satellite's 25-minute journey into an elliptical orbit, an on-board motor lofted it to a circular, geostationary orbit above Colombia.

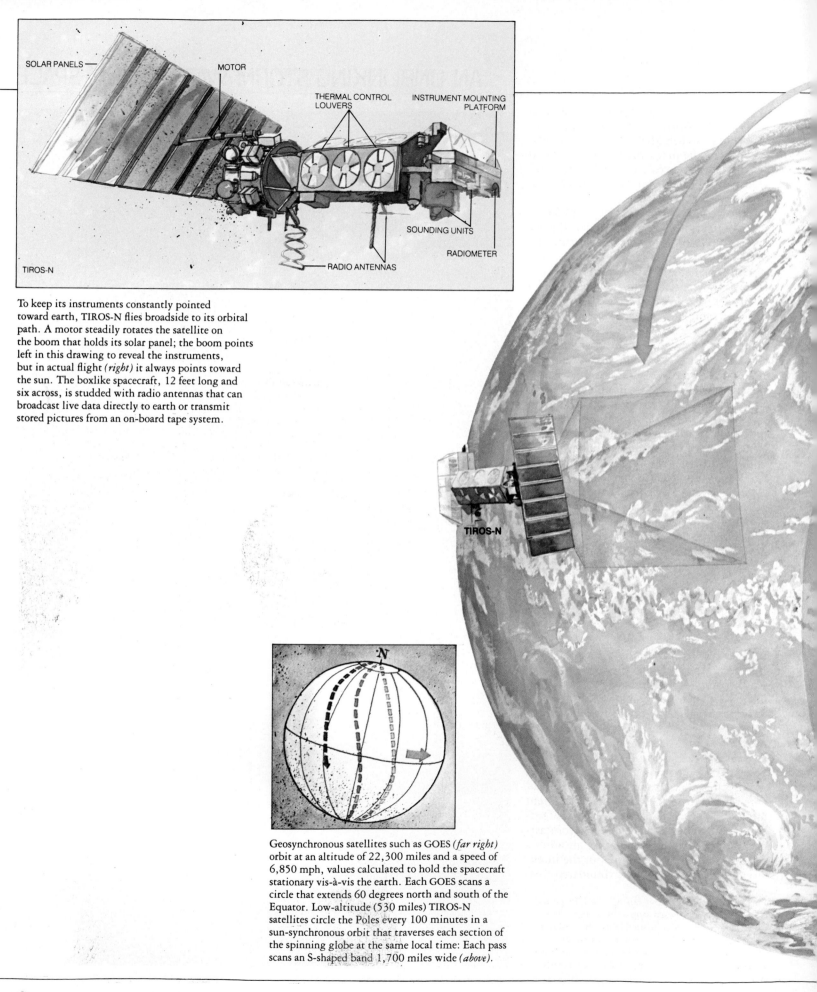

SOLAR PANELS

MOTOR

THERMAL CONTROL LOUVERS

INSTRUMENT MOUNTING PLATFORM

SOUNDING UNITS

RADIOMETER

RADIO ANTENNAS

TIROS-N

To keep its instruments constantly pointed toward earth, TIROS-N flies broadside to its orbital path. A motor steadily rotates the satellite on the boom that holds its solar panel; the boom points left in this drawing to reveal the instruments, but in actual flight *(right)* it always points toward the sun. The boxlike spacecraft, 12 feet long and six across, is studded with radio antennas that can broadcast live data directly to earth or transmit stored pictures from an on-board tape system.

TIROS-N

N

Geosynchronous satellites such as GOES *(far right)* orbit at an altitude of 22,300 miles and a speed of 6,850 mph, values calculated to hold the spacecraft stationary vis-à-vis the earth. Each GOES scans a circle that extends 60 degrees north and south of the Equator. Low-altitude (530 miles) TIROS-N satellites circle the Poles every 100 minutes in a sun-synchronous orbit that traverses each section of the spinning globe at the same local time: Each pass scans an S-shaped band 1,700 miles wide *(above)*.

SOLAR PANELS

RADIAL THRUSTERS

RADIOMETER
SUNSHADE

RADIOMETER

DESPUN SECTION

MAGNETOMETER

RADIO ANTENNAS

GOES-EAST

The GOES spins at 100 rpm on an axis parallel
to the earth's axis of rotation, both for stability and
scanning efficiency; a motor mechanically despins
the antenna module so that radio antennas always
point toward the satellite's ground station. The
spinning radiometer photographs nearly one quarter
of the earth's surface every 18 minutes, scanning a
five-mile band with each revolution; smaller sectors
can be photographed more quickly.

GOES-EAST

name of Skyfire, seeded Montana clouds with silver iodide on the theory that the chemical might increase the leakage current between charge centers and thereby reduce the number, duration or intensity of lightning flashes. At best, the results were statistically insignificant; at worst, or so it was suggested, silver iodide seeding might even increase the electrical activity within clouds.

A somewhat more promising technique applied in the 1970s by the National Oceanic and Atmospheric Administration was inspired by the experience of Allied bombing crews in World War II. By dropping litters of aluminum-coated thread fibers, known as chaff, the fliers could disrupt the electronic signals of enemy radar. Years later, tests in NOAA laboratories indicated that about five pounds—or 10 million fibers—of chaff, if spread through a thundercloud, might short-circuit the electrical force of lightning before it built up enough charge to make contact with the ground. The result, rather than destructive bolts of lightning, might be a steady but harmless electrical flow, or coronal discharge of the sort known as St. Elmo's fire. The idea made sense—but it met with limited success in the field, and funds for the project dried up.

Thus, by the late 1970s, the status of storm modification was best summarized at a 1978 meeting of the American Association for the Advancement of Science by Professor Dean E. Mann of the University of California at Santa Barbara: "The lightning suppression program is virtually dead, hail suppression has undergone retrenchment, major efforts at hurricane modification have been delayed." For scientists who still aspire to moderating the furies of storm, Mann added, "the frustration level is high."

Moreover, and perhaps of surpassing significance, the enthusiasm that pervaded early efforts at storm moderation had been diluted by doubts as to the basic wisdom of attempting to tinker with the world's weather. Storms—from hurricanes and typhoons to isolated thunderheads—were increasingly viewed as nature's vehicles for distributing heat around the planet. Throughout most of the earth's existence, global climate has varied widely between ice-age eons and periods too warm to permit the formation of permanent polar icecaps. Some scientists believe that these extremes are the most natural conditions of planetary climate, and that mankind now lives in an era of precarious balance between cataclysmic melting and freezing. Typifying the fears of such scientists, Gordon Dunn, retired director of the National Hurricane Center in Miami, wrote: "If hurricane control were successful and none were allowed to go through their full life cycle, nature would undoubtedly find some other method of maintaining the heat balance—and who can say that this new method might not be even more disastrous than the hurricane?"

Until such questions were at least partially answered, and until reasonable qualms could be overcome, it seemed likely that the most gainful approach to storm hazard still lay in research and in perfecting the science of forecasting.

At Camp Springs, Maryland, just south of Washington, D.C., stands the World Weather Building, a drab brown structure whose nondescript exterior conceals the sorcerer's world that lies within. This is the home of the National Meteorological Center. As such, it is both the hub of weather forecasting in the United States and a vital part of the global network established by no fewer than 120 nations, many of them normally at arm's length in their other relationships, to follow storms from birth to death.

From the remote and alien regions of outer space, from the contorted crusts of the earth's land masses, from the oceans that act as incubators for the embryos of giant storms, meteorological information flows in staggering magnitude. During each 24-hour period, the National Meteorological Center routinely receives 50,000 reports from surface stations, 2,500 radiosonde balloon readings from the upper atmosphere, 3,000 communications from ships sailing international sealanes and 3,200 more from aircraft patrolling the clouded skies; orbiting space

Labels on diagram:
"HARD HAT" TEMPERATURE SENSOR

ELECTRICAL PROBE

WIND-DIRECTION VANE

BAROGRAPH AIR-PRESSURE SENSOR

WIND-SPEED SENSOR

INTERNAL BATTERY

INKLESS RECORDERS

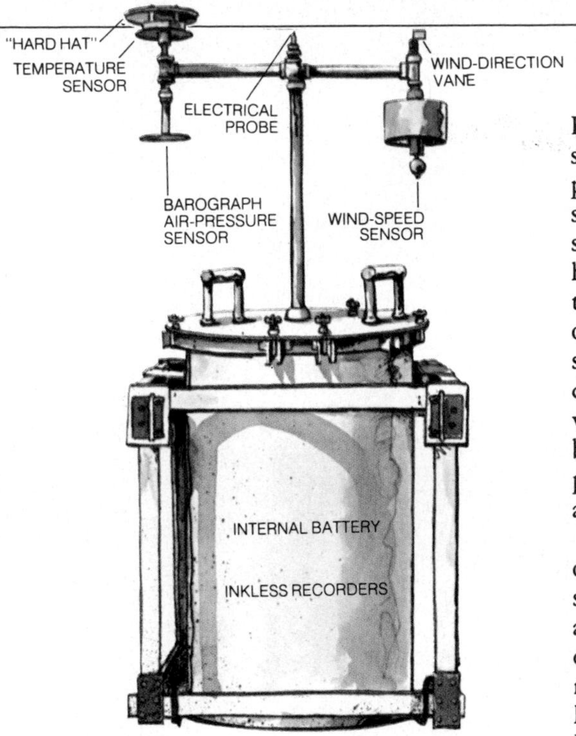

The Totable Tornado Observatory is a rugged cylindrical package of instruments designed to be carried into the path of a twister. It weighs 400 pounds and can operate in winds of up to 200 mph.

Precisely what goes on inside a tornado is still a mystery—and for good reason. So powerful are these brief, narrowly focused storms that direct measurements of wind speed, air pressure and electrical discharge have always been impossible to obtain. On those occasions when a twister has enveloped weather recording devices, it has destroyed both the instruments and their data. Scientific knowledge of the inner workings of a funnel cloud has thus been based on indirect evidence: Doppler radar pictures, photogrammetric film analysis and engineering studies of damage.

But a recent invention by two scientists of the U.S. National Oceanic and Atmospheric Administration, Alfred J. Bedard and Carl Ramzy, may change all this. Their creation—dubbed TOTO for Totable Tornado Observatory, but also in honor of the little dog who tackled a tornado in *The Wizard of Oz*—is a supersturdy, battery-operated weather station that can be transported directly into the path of a twister by a pickup truck. Bedard got the idea at a NOAA severe-storms conference in Norman, Oklahoma, where he learned about the work of teams who pursue thunderstorms in instrumented vans.

TOTO looks like a barrel with arms. Its casing is made of half-inch aluminum set in an angle-iron frame for stability. A wind-direction vane and a wind-speed sensor without moving parts are fitted to one arm. The other arm holds a temperature sensor with a "hard hat" hail shield and a special rapid response barograph to measure drastic air pressure changes. Between the arms is a probe to record electrical discharge. All the sensors are held in place by galvanized iron pipes that route electrical connections to electronic modules inside, where inkless recorders plot the readings.

When a tornado is sighted, a two-man crew drives into its path; TOTO is rolled out of the pickup on ramps and hoisted upright. The process takes only 20 seconds—and the recorders and sensors activate automatically as the TOTO team speeds away to safety.

satellites contribute 1,300 readings and 100 photographs, while weather radar stations add another 3,000 reports.

Within four hours after a piece of data has been received by one participating nation, it has been exchanged and is being shared by all. The radiosonde tracings of high-altitude air streams over the Philippines, or reports from flying laboratories based on the U.S. territory of Guam, may tell of a Pacific typhoon, and presage the activation of a highly effective Hong Kong typhoon warning system.

The task of assimilating and analyzing the torrents of information in time to warn of developing storms is beyond human capacity. A single forecast may involve several million bits of data and billions of mathematical calculations. Thus, in the United States, huge computers that can handle tens of millions of instructions per second come into constant play. The computer models for storm profiles have steadily been refined: In the early 1970s, the model for the Northern Hemisphere had 2,500 grid points, each 186 miles apart, with calculations for six different atmospheric levels; by 1980, the model was based on a grid of 3,648 points, each 104 miles apart, with calculations programed for 12 levels.

To feed the insatiable appetites of the computers, meteorologists have come to rely on weather satellites so sophisticated as to relegate earlier models to the horse-and-buggy era. In 1980, the United States had in orbit two Geostationary Operational Environmental Satellites (GOES), their paths so synchronized with the planet's rotation as to place them on permanent station above particular points on the earth's surface. One GOES satellite kept watch on hurricane development in the eastern United States and Canada, the Caribbean and South America and much of the Atlantic, while the other kept its instrumental eyes on the western half of the United States and Canada, along with much of the eastern Pacific. Still another geostationary satellite, dubbed Himawari-II ("sun-

A scene of serene majesty greets the crewmen of a
U.S. Air Force weather plane 10,000 feet above the
South China Sea as they enter the eye of Typhoon
Sarah in October 1979. By taking navigational fixes
within the eye, weathermen learn in which
direction the storm is headed and at what speed.

flower") by its fond owners, was put up by Japan in 1980 to watch over the western Pacific as far south as New Zealand. Meteosat-2, a product of the European Space Agency, guarded the eastern Atlantic. The United States also employed two satellites that circled the globe on a path over the North and South Poles from which they could photograph any weather formation on earth (*pages 155-157*).

Beyond the now-familiar images of the earth and its covering clouds, the modern weather satellites record atmospheric temperatures and the amount, distribution and motion of water vapor at various atmospheric levels. Transmitted to earth, the satellite information is relayed to a bank of minicomputers in the World Weather Building, where wondrous tricks are performed. Full-disc satellite images can be resolved to highly detailed close-ups covering half-mile sectors of cloud or ground; lines representing state or national boundaries can be superimposed on the images, which are then sent automatically to the areas that may be threatened by storms; varying temperatures within cyclonic clouds can be represented by different color shadings.

Even as the satellites maintain their unblinking gaze from outer space, the airborne human hurricane hunters are still hard at work—and they are better equipped than ever to invade the inner realms of the great storms and take quantitative measurements of their formation, motion and intensity. In 1977, three heavy-duty turboprop weather planes monitored Hurricane Anita as it roared across the Gulf of Mexico from August 30 through September 2. During one period, a weather plane remained within the storm for a full eight hours. Armed with the most advanced equipment, it measured the location and amount of rainfall and was able to make three-dimensional pictures of the storm every seven seconds. The result, according to one weather official, was "the best radar data ever recorded in a mature hurricane."

Such efforts obviously add to the sum of man's knowledge and enhance his forecasting abilities. Yet no single source of information, human or instrumental, is sufficient unto itself. To achieve success in the long struggle to foretell the behavior of storms, all resources must be gathered in full array. A dramatic example of the necessary interplay was found in the 1979 monitoring of Hurricane Frederic.

Forming hard on the heels of a gigantic hurricane that had been designated David, Frederic at first seemed insignificant. In early September it lingered weakly around Cuba, seemingly unable to decide whether to move or simply die away. Finally it teetered off to the west and entered the Gulf of Mexico—

An advisory posted at the entrance to the Star Ferry, which links the island of Hong Kong with Kowloon on the mainland, warns a passerby that a typhoon is approaching. Such advisories, along with continuous radio and television alerts, have kept loss of life to a minimum in Hong Kong, even though the British colony is located in an area known locally as Typhoon Alley.

where satellite reports showed it was gaining strength in alarming proportion.

By September 11, Frederic loomed large and lethal in the Gulf 350 miles southeast of Pensacola, Florida, well outside land-based radar range but the subject of avid attention from meteorologists who only a few days before had been following David. That evening, additional information from satellites, radar and airborne reconnaissance prompted the National Hurricane Center in Miami to issue a hurricane watch placing Frederic's probable landfall somewhere along a 290-mile stretch between Panama City, Florida, and New Orleans.

With all available human and technological resources now focusing on Frederic, it became clear that the huge hurricane was heading toward Mobile Bay, along whose heavily populated shores a storm surge could cost thousands of lives. "Each bay," one scientist later explained, "has its own particular set of characteristics, including its specific irregularly shaped coastline and sea floor, which influence how water flows in and out of the estuary." And though Mobile Bay had not been severely stricken by a hurricane since 1926, the National Oceanic and Atmospheric Administration was prepared for the dire eventuality. Stored in its computers were countless facts and figures about the bay's complex coastal and sea-floor configuration. Given Frederic's force, the computers could use the model of the bay to calculate the level of storm surge.

Within minutes after relevant data was fed in, the computer answer came: Hurricane Frederic's highest surge, striking near Gulf Shores, Alabama, approximately 50 miles southeast of Mobile, would reach about 12 feet. On the basis of that reckoning, and with almost equally fearsome tides forecast for other coastal areas, more than 250,000 persons were evacuated on September 12.

As it turned out, Hurricane Frederic, with winds of up to 145 miles per hour, struck within 35 miles of the predicted place, accompanied by a storm surge that averaged 12 feet—exactly as forecast. In terms of property damage, which came to an estimated $2.3 billion, it was the most costly hurricane in U.S. history. Yet thanks to timely warning, only five persons were killed.

The forecast of Frederic's landfall was well within the acceptable range of error, which by then had been narrowed to 100 miles, an improvement of 10 per cent during the decade of the 1970s. In its forecasts for all types of weather, the National Weather Service in 1980 had achieved an accuracy of 85 per cent for periods of up to 48 hours; beyond that, the chances diminished rapidly.

Indeed, for all the advances since Theophrastus listened to the baying of wolves and watched the rise of the sun, mankind is still far from fathoming the full nature of storm. And though high technology holds huge promise for the future, the present state of the science was vividly described by Vilhelm Bjerknes, son and grandson of the men of Bergen who founded modern meteorology and himself a meteorologist: "We are in the position of the physicist watching a pot of water coming to a boil. He knows intimately all the processes of energy transfer, molecular kinetics and thermodynamics involved. He can describe them, put them in the form of formulas and tell you a great deal about how much heat will boil how much water.

"Now ask him to predict precisely where the next bubble will form." **Ω**

SETTING A SNARE FOR A SUPERSTORM

Scientists are in basic agreement about what causes the precipitation in thunderstorms. But effective forecasting requires an understanding of why one storm may bring nourishing rains while another punishes the landscape with destructive flash floods, high winds, hail, lightning, even tornadoes. Cracking this mystery could make possible not only improved forecasting, but reliable cloud seeding techniques as well.

Unfortunately, most investigations have been hindered by the sheer immensity of these complex weather systems. An ordinary thunderhead contains some 2,000 cubic miles of swirling particles that interact in a bewildering array of physical and chemical phenomena. Field and laboratory studies have yielded many hypotheses, but few answers; each individual approach, says one meteorologist, "is like trying to attack a very large animal with a very small net."

In the summer of 1981, the U.S. government organized a thunderstorm research project whose size and complexity invited comparison with its subject. The Cooperative Convective Precipitation Experiment—acronymically known as CCOPE, and documented here and on the following pages—mobilized 200 scientists from 29 institutions and set up a headquarters in Miles City, Montana, the heart of the High Plains thunderstorm country. The scientists were armed with a satellite-linked network of 125 ground-level weather stations, eight advanced radars, five sophisticated upper-air sounding balloon stations and a fleet of 14 specially instrumented aircraft to fly in and around the storm systems. Their mission: to develop an accurate and comprehensive picture of the precipitation processes during the birth, life and death of a thunderstorm.

Between May and August, the scientists conducted 244 experiments in the area around Miles City, and obtained 5,000 computerized tapes, each containing some 25 million pieces of information. The analysis of this data yielded a wealth of information, but left the ultimate answers tantalizingly out of reach. As one of the project's top scientists put it: "In this business, there's never a final step. You answer some questions, and you open up new ones."

Pilots race to their aircraft as a thunderhead rolls across Montana toward the Miles City airport on August 2, 1981. Eight planes, part of the CCOPE research program, penetrated the cloud repeatedly to measure its water content, temperature and wind velocity at several altitudes.

A lancelike wind sensor on the nose of a twin-engined plane was designed to reach ahead of in-flight turbulence from the fuselage and propellers. The boom was internally fitted with an inertial navigation unit to subtract the aircraft's motion from the wind measurements.

The twin pods of a cloud particle measuring device jut from underneath the wing of a Cessna Citation jet. As the aircraft flew through thunderstorms, a laser beam, projected from one pod to a receptor cell on the other, detected the dimensions of cloud particles.

Under an overcast sky, a portable, solar-powered weather station instrumented to measure ground-level air pressure, humidity, wind speed and rainfall stands in a Montana wheat field. A dense network of such units covering 27,000 square miles telemetered readings every 60 seconds.

A meteorologist hauls a helium-filled weather balloon, known as a rawinsonde, from its storage shed toward the launch pad. Equipped with sensors and a radio transmitter, the rawinsondes measured data on horizontal wind fields as well as temperature and humidity in the upper air.

Inside a trailer beside a weather station, a scientist studies a print-out showing surface wind directions. The network of ground stations measured the atmospheric environment under the thunderstorms.

In the CCOPE control room, an operations director tracks a storm on a video console, using data from all the observing techniques, while other operators monitor aircraft and Doppler radar scannings.

SABRELINER
28,000 feet

KING AIR
20,000 feet

AERO COMMANDER
16,000 feet

SCHWEIZER SAILPLANE
16,000 to 28,000 feet

T-28
16,000 feet

QUEEN AIR
13,000 feet

QUEEN AIR
8,500 feet

Printed and bound in Italy by
A. Mondadori, Verona.
Depósito Legal: M - 20200 - XXX.